Emily Dickinson
A Bibliography: 1850-1966

Emily Dickinson

A Bibliography: 1850-1966

By Sheila T. Clendenning
San Fernando Valley State College

The Kent State University Press

The Serif Series:
Bibliographies and Checklists

William White, General Editor
Wayne State University

Library of Congress Card Catalogue Number 67-65585
Manufactured in the United States of America
at the press of The Oberlin Printing Company
Designed by Merald E. Wrolstad

First Edition

Preface

The present volume undertakes to provide students, teachers, and scholars with a bibliography which will be useful as a guide to research into the life and writings of Emily Dickinson. Previous bibliographies, those compiled by The Jones Library, Inc. and by Alfred Leete Hampson, were incomplete and eccentric even when they were published in 1930; today they are clearly obsolete. Consequently, this new bibliography aims to be a complete catalogue of: (1) editions of Emily Dickinson's writings, (2) first or early printings of her poems, (3) books, chapters in books, and parts of chapters, (4) bibliographies and bibliographical discussions, (5) unpublished doctoral dissertations and important M.A. and undergraduate theses, (6) essays and parts of essays published in periodicals, both scholarly and popular, (7) review articles, operationally defined as reviews extending to three or more pages. Though completeness is claimed only for items from the United States, England, and Canada, numerous foreign publications are included. And though the scope of the bibliography is nominally from 1850 to 1966, many 1967 contributions are included.

The bibliography is arranged in six sections as indicated in the Table of Contents. In all except Section II, the items are arranged alphabetically by author; within a run of two or more works by the same author the items are arranged alphabetically by title. In cases of works by two or more authors the items are arranged as if the first-listed author were the sole author. In cases of two or more works having the same author and identical titles the items are arranged chronologically by date of publication. Untitled articles within a run of two or more works by the same author are placed at the end of his titled articles; two or more untitled articles by the same author are arranged alphabetically by journal title. Anonymous headings within each section are filed as if "Anonymous" were the author's name. In Section II, part A is arranged alphabetically by editor; part B is arranged chronologically; part C is arranged first alphabetically by language, then alphabetically by translator.

The style of entry follows, with necessary modifications, that of the *MLA International Bibliography.* Each entry has its identifying number which is used for cross-reference and in the indexes. Numbers, however, which are preceded by a "J." refer to Dickinson poems as designated by Thomas H. Johnson in his edition (47). Cross-references are used to guide the user from books to their reviews and back, and to identify items in dialogue with other items. Whenever possible, reprints of chapters and articles are listed with full bibliographical data, but when separate publications are judged to be identical or nearly identical, they are given a single identifying number and listed according to the date of the first publication.

I am deeply grateful to my friend and teacher James L. Woodress who introduced me to Emily Dickinson and who advised and encouraged me in compiling this bibliography and to Vinton Dearing under whose tutelage this work was first begun. I am further indebted to the libraries of the University of California at Los Angeles, the University of California at Berkeley, Yale University, Harvard University, and Wesleyan University. Among the many librarians and publishers who have offered assistance, Charles R. Green and Winifred D. Sayer of The Jones Library, Inc., C. T. Laughter of Amherst College Library, Margaret S. Grierson of Smith College Library, Frances Benedict of Little, Brown and Company, Anne E. Williams of the Williston Memorial Library of Mount Holyoke College, and Charlotte Oyer of San Fernando Valley State College Library deserve special thanks. My gratitude goes also to my department chairman, Professor Harry Finestone, for his encouragement and to Professor Yoshinobu Hakutani, who provided several translations into Japanese.

But my warmest thanks go to my husband, John Clendenning, who has been by turns, baby sitter, chauffeur, typist, research assistant, critic, my comforter, my Ford Foundation.

Sheila T. Clendenning

San Fernando Valley State College
Northridge, California
August, 1967

Contents

Introduction: Emily Dickinson's Editors, Biographers, and Critics

The history of Emily Dickinson's literary reputation is, in a sense, a miniature chronicle of the development of American literary scholarship and criticism from 1890 to the present. In Dickinson's case, the history falls roughly into three periods. The first might be called "The Period of Todd and Higginson," after her first editors. It begins with the initial volume of Dickinson's verse, published posthumously in 1890. Mabel Loomis Todd, the wife of an Amherst professor, had undertaken the job of editing at the request of Lavinia and Austin Dickinson, the poet's sister and brother. Thomas Wentworth Higginson was brought in because of his distinguished reputation as editor and critic, but more important, because he had been Miss Dickinson's friend and literary advisor. To the amazement of Todd and Higginson, the first edition was quickly sold out, and while *Poems by Emily Dickinson* (54) went through numerous printings, the two editors set to work preparing *Poems, Second Series* (55) for publication the following year. Then, working by herself, Mrs. Todd edited *Letters of Emily Dickinson* (53) in 1894 and *Poems, Third Series* (56) in 1896, thus bringing to a close the period of Todd and Higginson.

It has become fashionable for twentieth century critics to deride these early editors for an unfaithful reproduction of the poems. Certainly the value of a reliable text cannot be exaggerated, but Todd and Higginson were in the unenviable predicament of being nineteenth century critics with packets of twentieth century poems to present to a nineteenth century audience. The editors were wise enough to think the poems good, and practical enough to realize that many of their contemporaries would find the poetry offensive in style, if not in content. Indeed, Thomas Niles of Roberts Brothers publishing firm made "creative editing" a condition of publication. Consequently, the two editors attempted to smoothe the meter and mend the rhyme for the sake of Emily and her audience.

And Todd and Higginson's sense of forboding proved correct. Among the great numbers of reviews in magazines and newspapers throughout the United States and Britain one criticism predominated: Emily Dickinson's form was a catastrophe; she could not spell, punctuate, rhyme, or scan! With the notable exception of William Dean Howells (588) and a few others, even the critics who praised her work—and these were certainly in the majority—were obliged to acknowledge that she lacked technical skill. Like Higginson (54), they defended her by denying that technique had much significance when balanced against Dickinson's inspiration and imagination. This was the birth of Emily Dickinson, Ariel of Amherst.

The period, then, from 1890 to 1913, viewed in general terms, was one in which the Dickinson cannon was first presented to its audience. And that audience was of a peculiarly nineteenth century turn of mind: it included many of Howells' young ladies; it avidly consumed magazines; it was shocked by technical innovation in poetry, but on the whole, entranced by the powers of imagination; it preferred a smooth to an accurate text.

"The Period of Bianchi," from 1914 to 1930, is likewise one of textual corruption, but of a different sort. Martha Dickinson Bianchi, daughter of Sue and Austin Dickinson, became embroiled, like her mother before her, in "The Dickinson Feud."

This well-known family squabble began soon after Mrs. Todd and Mr. Higginson began editing the manuscripts. Sue Dickinson, finding she was never consulted in the proceedings, became increasingly hostile toward the participants. The whole affair was climaxed by a famous lawsuit by Sue against Mrs. Todd; the story is described in detail by Mrs. Todd's daughter, Millicent Todd Bingham, in *Ancestors' Brocades* (171). But from the point of view of the scholar or devotee of Emily Dickinson, the crucial upshot of this otherwise ludicrous feud was that both the Todd and Sue Dickinson factions snapped the lid down tight on the unpublished manuscripts that each had.

In this second period, then, Mrs. Bianchi set out to present her Aunt Emily to the world. In 1914 she edited a collection of poems which were written to her mother, entitled *The Single Hound* (38). Then followed a whole series of editions: *The Complete Poems of Emily Dickinson* (32) in 1924; *The Life and Letters of Emily Dickinson* (35) in the same year; *Further Poems of Emily Dickinson: Witheld from Publication by Her Sister Lavinia* (34) in 1929; *The Poems of Emily Dickinson*, Centenary Edition (36) in 1930; *Emily Dickinson Face to Face: Unpublished Letters with Notes and Reminiscences by . . . Martha Dickinson Bianchi* (33) in 1932; *Unpublished Poems of Emily Dickinson* (39) in 1935; and *The Poems of Emily Dickinson* (37) in 1937. After producing what Mrs. Bianchi called a "complete" edition in 1924, she went on to edit no fewer than four new volumes of unpublished verse. By the reviewer who took the time to check, Mrs. Bianchi was upbraided for copying carelessly, for often printing a single poem as if it were two, and for badly arranging the poems.

Another editor of this period, Conrad Aiken, was called to the task both out of a recognition of the need for a comprehensive reading edition and out of a deep-seated horror at Mme. Bianchi's example. In 1924 he published his *Selected Poems of*

Emily Dickinson (28), deliberately using the older Todd-Higginson texts in preference to the newer editions. In 1929 he reviewed Bianchi's *Further Poems*, loosing a devastating broadside at her careless editing (348), and as late as 1945 he was still measuring with sardonic amusement the span of Mrs. Bianchi's ego (346). Aiken, then, ran directly counter to the temper of the second period. Not only did he oppose the method of editing, but he opposed as well the emphasis on the kind of biographical interest which was formulated in 1924 with Bianchi's *The Life and Letters of Emily Dickinson* (35) and culminated in the 1930 publication of Josephine Pollitt's *Emily Dickinson: The Human Background of Her Poetry* (198) and Genevieve Taggard's *The Life and Mind of Emily Dickinson* (205). Aiken reviewed both biographies (345), pointing with annoyance at their preoccupation with the Dickinson love myth and their use of conjecture as support for their hypotheses.

This emphasis on biography was also seen in the publication of a rash of personal reminiscences, usually in the form of an article or note, as in the case of Clara Bellinger Green's "A Reminiscence of Emily Dickinson" (551) and Gertrude Montague Graves' "A Cousin's Memories of Emily Dickinson" (549). But in one case, *Emily Dickinson: Friend and Neighbor* (187) by MacGregor Jenkins, the reminiscence reached book length. The Amherst children who had once danced about Miss Emily's skirts had grown up, not a little eager to help her frame her letter to the world. Distant relatives and Amherst graduates who had never seen her nevertheless had a word or two to contribute to the rapidly growing legend of the Nun of Amherst.

The second period, then, is principally one in which a series of new editions is produced, none of which is thoroughly reliable or complete, and a period of a perverse interest in biography, leading to endless gossip about the spinster's "lover," but rarely resulting in consideration of the relationship between

Dickinson's life and her artistic achievement. Essays of this period, for the most part, resemble those of the first period. That is, most are reviews, most are approving of Dickinson but tend to defend her by discounting the importance of technique in poetry, most criticize by epithet, calling her anything from the Gnome of Amherst to the American Sappho.

Yet this period is distinct from the first in one important aspect; it marks the beginning of a more serious kind of criticism. Viewing Dickinson's stylistic aberrations as possibly a conscious and important element of her style, a few critics began investigating, with varying degrees of success, her relationship to the literary world at large. Elizabeth Sergeant (791), for example, noted an affinity between Dickinson and the Imagists. Catherine Tolles (840) and Theodore Spencer (809) were struck by her similarities with the writers of the Metaphysical School; Genevieve Taggard compared her to John Donne (297). Allen Tate found her genius rooted in Puritan soil and assessed her impact on American literature (827), while Conrad Aiken examined her ties with Transcendentalism (347). Martha Hale Shackford considered Dickinson's techniques of the comic and the tragic (798). William Kelley compared her to Emily Brönte and delineated Dickinson's major themes as love, nature, death, and religion (265). Focusing closely on the work itself, Susan Miles described a relationship between Dickinson's form and content (680), while Francis Stoddard answered the charge of formlessness by explicating "I Died for Beauty" (818). Often these articles did not thoroughly investigate the questions they raised, but the questions, at least, were significant.

The third period, from 1931 to the present, is one of great scholarly and critical activity. Complaints about Mrs. Bianchi's editing and about the incomplete state of the *Complete Poems* had reached a terrible pitch by the close of the second period.

Two editors responded. Millicent Todd Bingham, Mabel Loomis Todd's daughter, once again lifted the lid of the legendary camphorwood chest and in 1945 published the carefully edited *Bolts of Melody* (51), a collection on which her mother was working before the feud began, and, in 1955, *Emily Dickinson's Home* (40), a collection of letters written by the poet and her family to Austin. As an aside in the Dickinson Feud, she published, also in 1945, *Ancestors' Brocades* (171), an interesting apologia for Todd and Higginson's editing practices in the early editions.

Welcome as these works were, the most significant contribution came in 1955 when Thomas H. Johnson published his three volume variorum edition of *The Poems of Emily Dickinson* (47). For the first time readers and scholars had before them a text carefully designed to be complete and reliable, containing variant readings of poems, tentatively arranged into a chronological order based on handwriting analysis. It is quite true that some new variants have been discovered since publication (104) and more than a few errors have been pointed out in the text and notes (631, 810, 929); still the edition represents a momentous step in Dickinson scholarship. The presentation of these volumes, together with the 1958 publication of *The Letters of Emily Dickinson* (46), co-edited by Theodora Ward, sparked a renaissance of interest and productivity in academic spheres. Consequently, Johnson deservedly gives his name in designating this third and final period.

Just as editing of "The Johnson Period" was a reaction against the editing of "The Bianchi Period," so too was biography a protest. The revolt against the maundering concern for Emily Dickinson's lovelife and the emphasis on the life at the expense of the work was signaled by the 1938 publication of *This Was a Poet: A Critical Biography of Emily Dickinson* (211) by George F. Whicher. His was the first biography to assume an important relationship existed between the life and the art. He addressed himself to the question of her religious and literary heritage: how she was influenced by Puritanism, by the Victorian poets, by Transcendentalists, by the tradition of American humor. Whicher's was the first rigorous attempt to sift fact from myth and to focus on the significant.

Curiously enough, however, even Whicher could not side-step the ubiquitous curiosity concerning the poet's lovelife. Based on the available facts and intelligent conjecture, Whicher's own theory emerged. The great love in Emily Dickinson's life was probably Wadsworth; her feelings were probably never articulated to him, much less consummated. Most critics today accept this account. However, Whicher made a contribution which is yet more valuable. For not only did he offer the most plausible answer to the question of the lover's identity, but he proceeded as well to discredit the whole inquiry by reminding readers that Dickinson herself had stipulated that the speaker in her poetry was a "supposed person." In other words, art was not synonymous with life.

But the world was not yet exorcised of its interest in Dickinson's lovelife. In 1951 Rebecca Patterson published *The Riddle of Emily Dickinson* (195), once again hanging out Emily's linen in a rarefied air of scholarly endeavor. Miss Patterson's sole purpose was to establish Kate Scott Anthon as Dickinson's lover; the poems were only considered insofar as they could be read as evidence of lesbianism. Angered by this last biography and its sister volumes of the previous period, in 1954 Mrs. Bingham retaliated by publishing *Emily Dickinson: A Revelation* (172), nominating her own candidate, Judge Lord, and offering as evidence the poet's letters to Lord. Like Whicher, Mrs. Bingham was both annoyed and intrigued with the question.

And the penchant for biographical gossip does not end here. But it is mitigated, at least, by an increasing analysis of the poems themselves and by a concern for offering valid and sufficient support for theses. Among the books considering themselves primarily biographical—though from this time on most books are both critical and biographical—Richard Chase's *Emily Dickinson* (177), published in 1951 is outstanding, particularly for its treatment of Puritanism's impact on Dickinson's mind and art. Thomas H. Johnson, turning in 1955 from editing to biography and criticism, published *Emily Dickinson: An Interpretive Biography* (188), containing important chapters on Dickinson's friends and presenting what may be the best existing guide to Dickinson's prosody. In 1961 Theodora Ward, Johnson's co-editor for the letters, likewise turned biographer, producing *The Capsule of the Mind: Chapters in the Life of Emily Dickinson* (209), a book which illuminates the relationship between Dickinson and T. W. Higginson and which examines letters and poems, tracing the poet's search for artistic objectivity. The only biography totally lacking in critical elements is nevertheless of real value. Jay Leyda's *The Years and Hours of Emily Dickinson* (190), a two volume work published in 1960, rather than being a true biography, is the raw material for biography—a cautious massing of facts about Dickinson's daily life presented in the form of a log. For as Leyda himself admits in the preface, he had been dismayed by the morass of myth surrounding Dickinson's life and wanted to clear the air. In other words, he was in direct reaction against biography of the second period.

Just as most of the biographies of this period are partly critical, so too are most of the critical books, in a sense, biographical. Many begin, like that of Henry W. Wells in *Introduction to Emily Dickinson* (210) and Douglas Duncan in *Emily Dickinson* (179), with a re-creation of Emily Dickinson's life in Amherst. But of those critics who do not begin in this way, who affirm with Clark Griffith (184) that since all the biographical data is in, we need not waste our time in endless repetition, most are concerned to some extent with her life as artist. Charles R. Anderson, for example, in *Emily Dickinson's Poetry: Stairway of Surprise* (170) is specifically concerned with Dickinson's views on art and the concept she had of herself as an artist. Similarly, David T. Porter in *The Art of Emily Dickinson's Early Poetry* (199) attempts to trace Dickinson's artistic development. In *Emily Dickinson: The Mind of the Poet* (182) Albert J. Gelpi investigates "the aesthetics of consciousness."

Books of this period likewise have in common a view of Emily Dickinson as a part of some intellectual or artistic tradition. Griffith's *The Long Shadow: Emily Dickinson's Tragic Poetry* (184), for example, examines Dickinson in relation to tragedy and romanticism, while Donald E. Thackrey in *Emily Dickinson's Approach to Poetry* (206) finds her rooted in mysticism.

Essays of this period reveal a similar approach. Dissatisfied with myth, with daydreams of youthful or aged lovers, with half-formed theories of inspiration, today's critic usually assumes that, recluse though she was, like all poets, Dickinson has both a social and a literary heritage.

Many of these essays examine Dickinson in terms of American traditions and institutions. Constance Rourke, for example, conceives of Dickinson's wit as part of the mainstream of Yankee humor (292). Many critics agree on Dickinson's connection with the Transcendentalists, and George F. Whicher has made a plausible suggestion that Emerson and Dickinson actually met (893). Roy Harvey Pearce denies she is a Transcendentalist but roots her in American soil as an exponent of the ego-centric style (283). Allen Tate finds American Puritanism, though in a state of disintegration, the ideal breeding-ground for the poet (828). Richard Chase has even designated her chief artistic failings as native in origin; they are examples of American rococo (466).

Some critics see Dickinson in terms of her relationship to the literary world at large. Her affinity with the Metaphysical School has been suggested more often than explored, but Henry W. Wells' "Frugality and Infinity" (320) is a valuable introduction. Louise Bogan, among several others, considers Dickinson's Mystical qualities, focusing on her similarities with William Blake (221). In terms of imagery and structure, Suzanne M. Wilson finds Dickinson, the French Symbolists, and Japanese Haiku poets in sympathy (911).

Like the books of this period, the essays often pursue questions of aesthetics and technique. Wilbur Merrill Frohock in "Emily Dickinson: God's Little Girl" (244), for example, investigates Dickinson's use of the child persona. Suzanne M. Wilson in "Structural Patterns in the Poetry of Emily Dickinson" (912) argues that Dickinson's organization usually follows that of the sermon. Frederic I. Carpenter, turning to questions of prosody, finds Dickinson's use of approximate rhyme reinforces meaning in her poetry (455). William Howard, impatient with unsupported remarks concerning Dickinson's vocabulary, supplies trustworthy ideas about her use of language by consulting a concordance and making careful tabulations (587). With a similar thoroughness, Rebecca Patterson in "Emily Dickinson's Palette" (731) examines the poet's developing use of color imagery.

What, then, is the general assessment of Dickinson scholarship over the past seventy-five years? It would be erroneous to conceive of an unempeded journey down the ringing grooves of change. We still retreat into exclamation and epithet; we excitedly make discoveries that Howells made over seventy years ago and Whicher, nearly thirty; we cannot evade a primordial desire to peep behind Miss Dickinson's window shades. But we are armed now with Johnson's texts, Leyda's log, Rosenbaum's concordance, and a history of some excellent criticism among much that is flawed or irrelevant. We have, in short, the tools to seek the poet, Dickinson, and the wisdom to let the White Moth of Amherst fall where she may.

S. T. C.

Abbreviations of Periodicals

AAN	*Amherst Alumnae News*
AAQ	*Amherst Alumnae Quarterly*
ABC	*American Book Collector*
AGQ	*Amherst Graduates Quarterly*
AH	*American Heritage*
AI	*American Imago*
AION-SG	*Annali Istituto Universitario Orientale, Napoli, Sezione Germanica*
AL	*American Literature*
ALM	*Amherst Literary Monthly*
ALR	*American Literary Review*
AmerB	*Amerika Bengaku*
AmhMo	*Amherst Monthly*
AmhR	*Amherst Record*
AndQ	*Andean Quarterly*
AN&Q	*American Notes & Queries*
ASc	*American Scholar*
A Spec	*American Spectator*
AutA	*Autograph Album*
AveM	*Ave Maria*
AW	*Amherst Writing*
BA	*Bachelor of Arts*
BB	*Bulletin of Bibliography*

BBAAS	*Bulletin of the British Association for American Studies*
BCP	*Book Collector's Packet*
BET	*Boston Evening Transcript*
BG	*Boston Globe*
BH	*Boston Herald*
BLM	*Bonniers Litterära Magasin*
BM	*Brown Magazine*
BNYPL	*Bulletin of the New York Public Library*
BookB	*Book Buyer*
BosC	*Boston Courier*
BosP	*Boston Post*
BPLQ	*Boston Public Library Quarterly*
BSG	*Boston Sunday Globe*
BTGU	*Bulletin of Tokyo Gakugei University*
BuR	*Bucknell Review*
CanL	*Canadian Literature*
CathW	*Catholic World*
CCQ	*Colby College Quarterly*
CCW	*Congregationalist and Christian World*
CdS	*Corriere della Sera*
CE	*College English*
CEA	*CEA Critic*
CHA	*Cuadernos Hispano-Americanos* [Madrid]
Chel	*Chelsea*
ChiTrib	*Chicago Tribune*
ChriCent	*Christian Century*
ChrR	*Christian Register*
CJ	*Classical Journal*
CL	*Comparative Literature*
ClH	*Clearing House*
CLQ	*Colby Library Quarterly*
CMR	*Culture Monthly Review* [*Van-Hoá Nguyêt-San*]
Colop	*Colophon*

ColQ	*Colorado Quarterly*
Conv	*Convivium* [Italy]
COut	*Classical Outlook*
CQ	*Classical Quarterly*
CR	*Creative Reading*
CrB	*Critisch Bulletin*
CritQ	*Critical Quarterly*
CS	*Cahiers du Sud*
CSM	*Christian Science Monitor*
CurL	*Current Literature*
Cweal	*Commonweal*
DAM	*Dartmouth Alumnae Magazine*
DARM	*Daughters of the American Revolution Magazine*
DUJ	*Durham University Journal*
DW	*DerWesten*
EAA	*English "A" Analyst* [Northwestern University]
EJ	*English Journal*
EL	*Educational Leader*
ELeaf	*English Leaflet*
ELH	*Journal of English Literary History*
ELN	*English Language Notes*
ES	*English Studies* [Amsterdam]
E&S	*Essays and Studies by Members of the English Association*
ESQ	*Emerson Society Quarterly*
EurR	*Europäische Revue*
Expl	*Explicator*
FLe	*Fiera Letteraria*
Fre	*Freeman*
Gak	*Gakuen*
GaR	*Georgia Review*
GLB	*Godey's Lady's Book*
HH	*Hound & Horn*

Highl	*Highlights*
HLB	*Harvard Library Bulletin*
HM	*Harper's Magazine*
H&M	*Hommes et Mondes*
HopR	*Hopkins Review*
HornBk	*Hornbook*
Hort	*Horticulture*
HSELL	*Hiroshima Studies in English Language and Literature*
HudR	*Hudson Review*
ICUT	*Improving College and University Teaching*
IEY	*Iowa English Yearbook*
ILN	*Illustrated London News*
IQB	*Indiana Quarterly for Bookmen*
JA	*Jahrbuch Für Amerikastudien*
JAE	*Journal of Adult Education*
JEGP	*Journal of English and Germanic Philology*
JHGWJC	*Journal of Hokusei Gakuen Women's Jr. College*
KAL	*Kyusha American Literature*
Kam	*Kamereon*
KR	*Kenyon Review*
LA	*Living Age*
Land	*Landmark*
LCM	*Literary Criterion, Mysore*
LD	*Literary Digest*
Let	*Letteratura*
LonDN	*London Daily News*
LonMerc	*London Mercury*
MCR	*Melbourne Critical Review*
MdR	*Midwest Review*
Merkur	*Merkur {Deutsche Zeitschrift Für Europäisches Denken]*
Mes	*Mesures*

MGR	*Meiji-Gakuen Ronso*
MHAQ	*Mount Holyoke Alumnae Quarterly*
MinnR	*Minnesota Review*
MLN	*Modern Language Notes*
MM	*Midland Monthly*
Monatshefte	*Monatshefte Für Deutschen Unterricht, Deutsche Sprache und Literatur*
MQ	*Midwest Quarterly*
MR	*Massachusetts Review*
MSpr	*Moderna Språk* [Stockholm]
NA	*Nuova Antologia*
N&A	*Nation and Athenaeum*
NAR	*North American Review*
NC	*Nineteenth Century*
NEQ	*New England Quarterly*
NHQ	*New Hungarian Quarterly*
NL	*Nouvelles Litéraires*
NMQ	*New Mexico Quarterly*
N&Q	*Notes and Queries*
NR	*New Republic*
NRCrit	*Nouvelle Revue Critique*
NS	*Neueren Sprachen*
NS&N	*New Statesman and Nation*
NY	*New Yorker*
NYHTB	*New York Herald Tribune, Books*
NYTBR	*New York Times, Book Review Section*
Oob	*Ord Och Bild*
Outl	*Outlook*
Parn	*Parnasso*
Person	*Personalist*
PF	*Pace Filologiczne*
PG	*Popular Gardening*
PL	*Poet Lore*

PMLA	*Publications of the Modern Language Association of America*
PoR	*Poetry Review*
PP	*Parola del Popolo*
PR	*Partisan Review*
PrS	*Prairie Schooner*
PULC	*Princeton University Library Chronicle*
PUSA	*Perspectives U.S.A.*
PW	*Publishers' Weekly*
QJS	*Quarterly Journal of Speech*
QQ	*Queen's Quarterly*
QRL	*Quarterly Review of Literature*
RA	*Revue Anglo-Américaine*
RCC	*Revue des Cours et Conférences*
RDM	*Revue des Deux Mondes*
RdP	*Revue de Paris*
REL	*Review of English Literature*
Ren	*Renascence*
RLM	*Revue des Lettres Modernes*
RMR	*Rocky Mountain Review*
RNC	*Revista Nacional de Cultura* [Caracas]
RT	*Round Table*
SA	*Studi Americani* [Rome]
SAQ	*South Atlantic Quarterly*
SatR	*Saturday Review*
SRP	*Saturday Review of Politics, Literature, Science, and Art*
Schol	*Scholastic*
ScienR	*Scientific Researches*
SB	*Studies in Bibliography: Papers of the Bibliographical Society of the University of Virginia*
SCM	*Smith College Monthly*

Scr	*Scrutiny*
Scrib	*Scribner's*
SEL	*Studies in English Literature*
SH	*Studies in Humanities*
SN	*Studia Neophilologica*
SO	*Sunday Oregonian*
SoR	*Southern Review*
Spec	*Spectator*
SpringR	*Springfield Republican*
SpringU	*Springfield Union*
SR	*Sewanee Review*
StN	*St. Nicholas*
SUS	*Susquehanna University Studies*
SWR	*Southwest Review*
Sym	*Symposium*
TC	*Twentieth Century*
T&G	*Town and Gown*
TGM	*Theatre Guild Magazine*
TLS	[London] *Times Literary Supplement*
TSE	*Tulane Studies in English*
TSLL	*Texas Studies in Literature and Language*
UCC	*University of California Chronicle*
UCR	*Union College Review*
UKCR	*University of Kansas City Review*
UNCEB	*University of North Carolina Extention Bulletin*
URev	*University Review*
UTQ	*University of Toronto Quarterly*
VAM	*Vassar Alumnae Magazine*
VQR	*Virginia Quarterly Review*
WHR	*Western Humanities Review*
YC	*Youth's Companion*
YLM	*Yale Literary Magazine*

YR	*Yale Review*
YULG	*Yale University Library Gazette*

I. Bibliographies

1. Archibald, R. C. "Emily Dickinson: A Song." *N&Q*. CLXVI (1934), 71. [Lists an ED poem set to music.]
2. Babler, Otto F. "Emily Dickinson: A Bibliographical Note." *N&Q*, CLXV (1933), 29. [Lists a Czech translation of ED.]
3. Bingham, Millicent Todd. "Early Reviews of Books by Emily Dickinson, 1890-1896." In Number 171, pp. 406-411. [Supplements this bibliography.]
4. Birss, J. H. "Emily Dickinson: A Bibliographical Note." *N&Q*, CLXIV (1933), 421. [Lists an early anthologized poem.]
5. Blanck, Jacob. "Emily Elizabeth Dickinson." *Bibliography of American Literature*, II, pp. 446-454. New Haven: Yale University Press, 1957. [Descriptive, but incomplete. Supplements this bibliography by including poems set to music, anthologies, fiction.]
6. Clark, Harry H., ed. "Emily Dickinson." *Major American Poets*, pp. 894-897. New York: American Book Co., 1936. [Annotated. Not supplementary to this bibliography.]
7. Frump, Timothy. "Emily Dickinson: A Song." *N&Q*, CLXV (1933), 386. [Lists an ED poem set to music.]
8. Green, Charles R. "Poetry about Emily Dickinson," *BB*, XX (1951), 114-115. [Brief list supplementing Number 25.]

9. Guidetti, Paolo. "La Fortuna di Emily Dickinson en Italia (1933-1962)." *SA*, IX (1963), 121-172. [Bibliographical essay on ED's literary reputation in Italy. List of translations, critical articles. In Italian. Supplements this bibliography. Discussed in Number 17.]

10. Hampson, Alfred Leete. *Emily Dickinson: A Bibliography.* Northampton, Mass.: Hampshire Bookshop, 1930. [Makes no claim to be exhaustive. Not intended for scholars. Supplements this bibliography by listing poems set to music, brief reviews, poems to ED. Reviewed in Number 878.]

11. Hartwick, Harry. *A History of American Letters*, pp. 553-555. Walter F. Taylor, ed. Boston: American Book Co., 1936. [Enumerative. Not supplementary to this bibliography.]

12. The Jones Library, Inc. *Emily Dickinson, December 10, 1830-May 15, 1886: A Bibliography.* Foreword George F. Whicher. Amherst, Mass.: The Jones Library, Inc., 1930. [Not annotated or descriptive. Contains items supplementary to this bibliography, i.e., brief newspaper notices and reviews, poems set to music, poems written to ED, fictionalized biography, M.A. theses. Whicher's introd. reprinted in Number 174, pp. 137-141; touches on ED's literary reputation, Amherst's religious climate, ED as psychological poet, her technique, preoccupation with renunciation, and local color qualities.]

13. Kuntz, Joseph M. *Poetry Explication: A Checklist of Interpretations since 1925 of British and American Poems Past and Present*, pp. 71-79. Denver: A Swallow, 1962. [Not supplementary to this bibliography.]

14. Leary, Lewis Gaston. *Articles on American Literature, 1900-1950*, pp. 68-71. Durham, N.C.: Duke University Press, 1954. [Not supplementary to this bibliography.]

15. McCarthy, William H., Jr., comp. *Emily Dickinson: Catalogue of Centennial Celebration.* New Haven: Yale University Press, 1930. [An exhibition catalogue.]

16. Robbins, J. Albert. "Emily Dickinson." *American Literary Scholarship: An Annual, 1963*, pp. 126-128. James Woodress, ed. Durham, N.C.: Duke University Press, 1965. [Bibliographical essay discussing Numbers 203, 543, 763, 772, 812, 884, 912, 925.]

17. ———. "Emily Dickinson." *American Literary Scholarship: An Annual, 1964*, pp. 130-136. James Woodress, ed. Durham, N.C.: Duke University Press, 1966. [Bibliographical essay discussing Numbers 9, 174, 184, 189, 202, 494, 519, 545, 677, 731, 770, 905, 911, 940.]

18. ———. "Emily Dickinson." *American Literary Scholarship: An Annual, 1965*, pp. 153-159. James Woodress, ed. Durham, N. C.: Duke University Press, 1967. [Bibliographical essay discussing Numbers 179, 182, 421, 488, 510, 516, 517, 535, 621, 678, 751, 794, 865, 943.]

19. Smith, Russell St. Clair. "A Dickinson Bibliography." M.A. Thesis, Brown University, 1948. [Includes many categories not covered by this bibliography: poems set to music, anthologies, drama, fiction, poems to ED, brief reviews, newspaper clippings. Entries for editions are descriptive and list contents. Considerable annotation. Thin coverage of scholarly articles and books. Chronological organization and lack of index make locating specific items difficult.]

20. ———. "Emily Dickinson: A Bibliographical Note." *N&Q*, CXCIII (1948), 188-189. [Data on early printings of two ED poems.]

21. Spiller, Robert E., *et al.* "Emily Dickinson." *Literary History of the United States: Bibliography.* 3rd ed.: revised. vol. II, pp. 467-470; sup., pp. 105-107. New York: The

Macmillan Company, 1963. [Bibliographical essay. Thorough treatment of editions up to 1945. No items supplementary to this bibliography.]

22. Wells, Anna M. "Early Criticism of Emily Dickinson." *AL*, I (1929), 243-259. [Focuses on ED's literary reputation before turn of century, demonstrating ED was well known before 1900. Bibliographical data.]

23. Whicher, George F. "Bibliographical Postscript." In Number 211, pp. 311-329.

24. Whicher, Stephen E. "Swedish Knowledge of American Literature: A Supplementary Bibliography." *JEGP*, LVIII (1959), 666-671. [Not supplementary to this bibliography.]

25. White, William. "Homage to Emily Dickinson: Tributes by Creative Artists." *BB*, XX (1951), 112-115. [Includes poems to ED, musical arrangements, illustrations, plays, novels, a dance, a textile design. Supplemented by Number 8.]

26. ———. "Two Unlisted Emily Dickinson Poems." *CLQ*, Ser. III (1948), 69-70. [Offers supplements to Numbers 10 and 12. Identifies "A Clamour in the Treetops" and "If God upon the Seventh Day" as poems by ED published in Number 127. The authenticity of these poems has been disputed by Johnson, and they are not included in his editions (Numbers 44, 45, 47).]

27. Woodress, James. "Dickinson, Emily." *Dissertations in American Literature, 1891-1955, with Supplement, 1956-1961*, p. 12, sup. p. 88. Durham, N. C.: Duke University Press, 1962. [Not supplementary to this bibliography.]

II. Works by Emily Dickinson

A. Editions of Poems and Letters

28. Aiken, Conrad, ed. *Selected Poems of Emily Dickinson.* London: Jonathan Cape, 1924; New York: Modern Library, 1948; Toronto: Random House of Canada, 1948. [Introd. views ED in cultural context. ED and Emerson. Her views on God, nature, death. Reprinted in Numbers 174, pp. 110-117; 347, pp. 156-163. Reviewed in Number 690.]
29. Anonymous. *Eighteen Poems.* Northampton, Mass.: Apiary Press, 1957. [Gift volume. Limited edition.]
30. Anonymous. *Emily Dickinson: Love Poems and Others.* Mt. Vernon, N. Y.: Peter Pauper Press, 1950; London: Mayflower Publishing Company, Ltd., 1956; London: Vision Press, Ltd., 1956. [Text based on Todd and Higginson's Numbers 54, 55.]
31. Baskin, Esther, and Leonard Baskin, eds. *Riddle Poems: Emily Dickinson.* Northampton, Mass.: Gehenna Press, 1957. [A slim gift volume. Limited edition.]
32. Bianchi, Martha Dickinson, and Alfred Leete Hampson, eds. *The Complete Poems of Emily Dickinson.* London: Martin Secker, 1924; Boston: Little, Brown and Company, 1924. [Neither complete nor reliable. Reviewed in Numbers 428, 439, 527, 528, 774, 822.]

33. Bianchi, Martha Dickinson. *Emily Dickinson Face to Face: Unpublished Letters with Notes and Reminiscences by . . . Martha Dickinson Bianchi.* Boston: Houghton Mifflin Company, 1932. [Text and notes unreliable. Reviewed in Number 782.]
34. ——— and Alfred Leete Hampson, eds. *Further Poems of Emily Dickinson: Witheld from Publication by Her Sister Lavinia.* London: Martin Secker, 1929. [Introd. by Bianchi touches on ED and religion, seclusion, Higginson. Text unreliable. Reviewed in Numbers 309, 428, 502, 514, 569, 591, 716, 809, 848, 859, 875.]
35. Bianchi, Martha Dickinson, ed. *The Life and Letters of Emily Dickinson.* Boston: Houghton Mifflin Company, 1924; London: Jonathan Cape, 1924. [An early biography along with incomplete collection of letters, edited by ED's niece. Text, based on Todd's 1894 edition, contains numerous errors. For a devastating criticism see Number 778. Reviewed in Numbers 366, 413, 439, 527, 551, 618, 638, 768, 774, 822, 842.]

Bianchi, Martha Dickinson, and Alfred Leete Hampson, eds. *Poems by Emily Dickinson.* See Number 37.

36. ———. *The Poems of Emily Dickinson.* Centenary Edition. Boston: Little, Brown and Company, 1930; London: Martin Secker, 1933. [Collected previously published poems. Reviewed in Numbers 673, 761.]
37. ———. *The Poems of Emily Dickinson.* Boston: Little, Brown and Company, 1937; London: Jonathan Cape, Ltd., 1937. [Introd. by Hampson. Collects poems from Numbers 36, 38, 39; organizes by theme. Title of U.S. edition changes to *Poems by Emily Dickinson* in 1946, although no textual changes. British edition retains title. Has gone through twenty-two printings. Reviewed in Numbers 392, 558.]

38. Bianchi, Martha Dickinson, ed. *The Single Hound: Poems of a Lifetime.* Boston: Little, Brown and Company, 1914. [Poems written to Sue Dickinson with an introd. by her daughter. Reviewed in Numbers 575, 791.]
39. ——— and Alfred Leete Hampson, eds. *Unpublished Poems of Emily Dickinson.* Boston: Little, Brown and Company, 1935; Toronto: McClelland and Stewart, Ltd., 1936. [Reviewed in Numbers 309, 430, 647, 790.]
40. Bingham, Millicent Todd, ed. *Emily Dickinson's Home: Letters of Edward Dickinson and His Family with Documentation and Comment by Millicent Todd Bingham.* New York: Harper and Bros., 1955; Toronto: Musson Book Co., Ltd., 1955; N.Y.: Dover, 1967. [Letters by ED and family written to Austin Dickinson, set into social context. Reveals family relationships, gives multiple points of view on contemporary issues, relates daily minutiae. Chapter identifying correspondents and acquaintances. Reviewed in Numbers 552, 676, 803, 908.]

Bingham, Millicent Todd, ed. See also Numbers 51, 172.

41. Brinnin, John Malcolm, ed. *Emily Dickinson.* (The Laurel Poetry Series.) New York: Dell Publishing Company, Inc., 1960. [Selection of 173 poems. Text based on Bianchi-Hampson (Number 37), Todd-Bingham (Number 51), and Johnson (Number 47) editions. Regularized capitalization and punctuation. Introd. (pp. 7-20) emphasizes relationship between life and work, form, history of publication, ED's place in world literature.]
42. Dickinson, Emily. *Emily Dickinson Manuscripts Presented by Millicent Todd Bingham to Amherst College, 1956-1957.* [Microfilm, Folger Shakespeare Library, 1957. See Number 173.]
43. Hampson, Alfred Leete, ed. *Poems for Youth, by Emily Dickinson.* Boston: Little, Brown and Company, 1918;

Toronto: McClelland and Stewart, Ltd., 1934. [Children's edition. Foreword by May Lamberton Becker. Illustrated by George and Doris Hauman.]

44. Johnson, Thomas H. ed. *The Complete Poems of Emily Dickinson.* Boston: Little, Brown and Company, 1960; Toronto: Little, Brown and Company (Canada) Ltd., 1960. [A reading text with a single version of all known poems. Reviewed in Numbers 508, 610, 669, 684.]

45. ———. *Final Harvest: Emily Dickinson's Poems.* Boston: Little, Brown and Company, 1961; Toronto: Little, Brown and Company (Canada) Ltd., 1961. [Reading edition with selected texts based on Number 44. Introd. by Johnson called "The Vision and Veto of Emily Dickinson" touches on aesthetics, prosody, tragic view.]

46. ——— and Theodora Ward, eds. *The Letters of Emily Dickinson.* 3 vols. Cambridge, Mass.: The Belknap Press of Harvard University Press, 1958; Toronto: S. J. Reginald Saunders, Ltd., 1958; London: Oxford University Press, 1958. [Introd. by Johnson. Standard edition. Chronological organization. Also contains prose fragments, identification of correspondents, index. Reviewed in Numbers 357, 484, 486, 671, 685, 811, 846. See also Number 553.]

47. Johnson, Thomas H. ed. *The Poems of Emily Dickinson: Including Variant Readings Critically Compared with All Known Manuscripts.* 3 vols. Cambridge, Mass.: The Belknap Press of Harvard University Press, 1955; London: Oxford University Press, 1955; Toronto: S. J. Reginald Saunders, Ltd., 1955. [Reviewed in Numbers 358, 371, 398, 423, 447, 628, 631, 665, 681, 759, 810, 845, 849, 870, 908. This is the standard edition of ED's poems, widely acclaimed for its exactness and completeness. Chronological arrangement. Johnson's introd. includes (I,

xvii-xlviii) "Creating the Poems" (chiefly biographical) and "Editing the Poems: 1890-1945" (a review of previous editions). Also included (I, xlix-lix) is "Characteristics of the Handwriting" by Theodora Van Wagenen Ward. In addition there are eleven appendixes (III, 1189-1210): (1.) "Biographical Sketches of Recipients of Poems," (2.) "Tabulation of Recipients," (3.) "Tabulation of Poems Year by Year," (4.) "Unpublished Poems," (5.) "The Packets by Chronological Arrangement," (6.) "The Packets: The Todd Numbering," (7.) "Poems Duplicated in the Packets," (8.) "Titles of Poems Supplied by Emily Dickinson," (9.) "Poems Published in Emily Dickinson's Lifetime," (10.) "Chronological Listing of First Publication Elsewhere Than in Collections," (11.) Distribution of Missing Autographs." For a careful evaluation of this edition, see Number 929.]

48. Linscott, Robert N., ed. *Selected Poems and Letters of Emily Dickinson.* Garden City, N. Y.: Doubleday and Company, Inc. (Anchor Books), 1959; London: W. H. Allen and Company, Ltd., 1963. [Selection of 383 poems and 120 letters. Text of poems based on Todd-Higginson (Numbers 54, 55) and Todd (Number 56) editions. Reprints abridgement of Number 105.]

49. Plotz, Helen, ed. *Poems of Emily Dickinson.* New York: Thomas Y. Crowell, 1964. [Reading edition with drawings by Robert Kipniss, introd. by Plotz.]

50. Reeves, James, ed. *Selected Poems of Emily Dickinson.* New York: The Macmillan Company, 1959; London: William Heinemann, Ltd., 1959. [Based on Johnson text, with standardized punctuation, spelling. Extensive biographical and critical introd. reprinted in Number 203, pp. 117-126. Reviewed in Numbers 339 and 520.]

51. Todd, Mabel Loomis, and Millicent Todd Bingham, eds.

Bolts of Melody: New Poems of Emily Dickinson. New York: Harper and Brothers, 1945; London: Jonathan Cape, Ltd., 1945. [Foreword by Mark Van Doren. Introd. by Bingham. Arranged by theme. Spelling and punctuation regularized, but editing generally reliable. Reviewed in Numbers 250, 346, 377, 392, 431, 501, 518, 531, 546, 558, 568, 649, 670, 771, 796, 821, 823, 910, 915.]

52. Todd, Mabel Loomis, and T. W. Higginson, eds. *Emily Dickinson: Poems, First and Second Series.* Boston: Roberts Brothers, 1893; Cleveland: World Publishing Company, 1948; Toronto: McClelland and Stewart, Ltd., 1948. [Combines Numbers 54 and 55. Brief introd. in 1948 edition by Carl Van Doren; reprinted from Number 307. Reviewed in Number 126.]

53. Todd, Mabel Loomis, ed. *Letters of Emily Dickinson.* 2 vols. New York: Roberts Brothers, 1894; London and New York: Harper and Brothers, 1931; Cleveland: World Publishing Company, 1951; London: Gollancz, 1951; Toronto: McClelland and Stewart, Ltd., 1952; New York: Grosset and Dunlap, Inc., 1962. [The first edition of letters. Editing generally reliable, collection incomplete. Brief introd. by Todd. Mark Van Doren introduces 1951 edition. Harper edition reviewed in Numbers 126, 458, 695, 698, 781, 894; Gollancz edition reviewed in Number 758.]

54. Todd, Mabel Loomis, and T. W. Higginson, eds. *Poems by Emily Dickinson.* Boston: Roberts Brothers, 1890; London: James R. Osgood, McIlvaine and Company, 1891. [First published edition of ED's poetry. Higginson's introd. reprinted in Number 174, pp. 10-12. Brief presentation of ED as inspired but lacking in technique. Reviewed in Numbers 120, 121, 344, 349, 382, 385, 410, 623, 836.]

55. ———. *Poems by Emily Dickinson, Second Series.* Boston: Roberts Brothers, 1891. [Introd. by Todd discusses condition of MSS, handwriting and punctuation, problems in editing. Scattered biographical comment. Reprinted in Number 174, pp. 42-44. Reviewed in Numbers 122, 124, 388, 389, 783.]

56. Todd, Mabel Loomis, ed. *Poems by Emily Dickinson, Third Series.* Boston: Roberts Brothers, 1896. [Brief preface by Todd. Reviewed in Numbers 129, 453, 467.]

57. Untermeyer, Louis B., ed. *Emily Dickinson.* (The Pamphlet Poets.) New York: Simon and Schuster, 1927. [Brief introd. touching on biography, history of publication, style.]

58. ———. *Poems of Emily Dickinson, Selected and Edited by Louis Untermeyer.* New York: Limited Editions Club, 1952; New York: Heritage Press, 1952.

59. Ward, Theodora, ed. *Emily Dickinson's Letters to Dr. and Mrs. Josiah Gilbert Holland.* Cambridge, Mass.: Harvard University Press, 1951; Toronto: S. J. Reginald Saunders and Company, Ltd., 1951. [First publication of J.1266, J.1334, J.1336, J.1367, J.1606, J.1607. Reviewed in Numbers 458, 800. Introd. reprinted in Number 209, pp. 115-138. Revised.]

See also Numbers 97, 172, 178.

B. Poems and Letters Published in Journals and Anthologies

1. Works Published during Emily Dickinson's Life, Chronologically Arranged

60. [A prose valentine.] *The Indicator* (Amherst College), II (1850), 7. [ED's first published work. Probably sent to George H. Gould. Reprinted in Number 46.]
61. "A Valentine." *SpringR*, 20 Feb. 1852. [First publication of " 'Sic Transit Gloria Mundi' " (J.3).]
62. "The May-Wine." *SpringR*, 4 May 1861. [First publication of "I taste a liquor never brewed" (J.214). Badly edited version.]
63. "The Sleeping." *SpringR*, 1 March 1862, p. 2. [First publication of "Safe in their alabaster chambers" (J.216).]
64. "My Sabbath." *RT*, I (12 March 1864), 195. [First publication of "Some keep the Sabbath going to church" (J.324).]
65. "Sunset." *SpringR*, 30 March 1864. [First publication of "Blazing in gold and quenching in purple" (J.228).]
66. "The Snake." *SpringR*, 14 Feb. 1866. [First publication of "A narrow fellow in the grass" (J.986).]
67. "Success." *A Masque of Poets*, p. 174. Boston: Roberts Bros., 1878. [First publication of "Success is counted sweetest" (J.67). For the story behind this anthology, see Numbers 813 and 814. See also Number 914.]

2. First Posthumous Publication, Chronologically Arranged

a. Poetry

68. "Renunciation." *Scrib*, VIII (1890), 240. [First publication of "There came a day at summer's full" (J.322).]

69. Higginson, Thomas Wentworth, ed. "An Open Portfolio." *ChrU*, XLII (1890), 392-393. [Precedes the first edition of poems. Publishes J.58, J.98, J.139, J.172, J.187, J.193, J.216, J.266, J.321, J.441, J.449, J.524, J.619, J.1052; reprints J.216. Brief and appreciative commentary. Reprinted in Number 174, pp. 3-10; *American Poetry and Poetics: Poems and Critical Documents from the Puritans to Robert Frost*, pp. 417-426. Daniel G. Hoffman, ed. Garden City, N. Y.: Anchor Books, 1962.]
70. "Poems by the Late Emily Dickinson." *Independent*, XLIII (5 Feb. 1891), 1. [First publication of "Went up a year this evening" (J.93), "I held a jewel in my fingers" (J.245), "God made a little gentian" (J.442).]
71. "Two Lyrics by the Late Emily Dickinson." *Independent*, XLIII (12 March 1891), 1. [First publication of "Just lost when I was saved" (J.160) and "Through the strait pass of suffering" (J.792).]
72. "Morning." *StN*, XVIII (May, 1891), 491. [First publication of "Will there really be a 'Morning' " (J.101).]
73. "The Sleeping Flowers." *StN*, XVIII (June, 1891), 616. [First publication of "Whose are the little beds, I asked" (J.142).]
74. "Vanished." *YC*, LXV (25 Aug. 1891), 420. [First publication of "She died—this was the way she died" (J.150).]
75. "A Nameless Rose." *YC*, LXIV (1891), 672. [First publication of "Nobody knows this little rose" (J.35).]
76. "Nobody." *Life*, XVII (1891), 146. [First publication of "I'm nobody! Who are you" (J.288).]
77. "A Poem." *ChrR*, LXX (1891), 212. [First publication of "God is a distant, stately lover" (J.357).]
78. "Autumn." *YC*, LXV (1892), 448. [First publication of "The name of it is 'Autumn' " (J.656).]
79. "In September." *YC*, LXV (1892), 484. [First publication of September's baccalaureate" (J.1271).]

80. "Saturday." *YC*, LXV (1892), 468. [First publication of "From all the jails the boys and girls" (J.1532).]
81. "Heart's-Ease." *YC*, LXVI (1893), 256. [First publication of "I'm the little 'Heart's Ease' " (J.176).]
82. "My Little King." *YC*, LXVI (1893), 256. [First publication of "I met a king this afternoon" (J.166).]
84. Howe, M. A. De Wolfe, ed. "Literary Affairs in Boston." *BookB,* XI (1894), 425. [First publication of "They might not need me, yet they might" (J.1391).]
85. "Time's Healing." *Independent*, XLVIII (21 May 1896), 1. [First publication of "They say that 'Time assuages' " (J.686).]
86. "Parting: My Life Closed Twice before Its Close." *Scrib*, XIX (June, 1896), 780. [First publication of J.1732.]
87. "Verses by Emily Dickinson." *Independent*, XLVIII (2 July 1896), 1. [First publication of J.747, J.1203, J.1547, J.1736.]
88. "Three Poems by Emily Dickinson." *Outl*, LIII (1896), 140. [First publication of J.466, J.501, J.1083.]
89. "Nature's Way." *YC*, LXXII (20 Jan. 1898), 36. [First publication of "Were nature mortal lady" (J.1762).]
90. "Fame." *Independent*, L (3 Feb. 1898), 1. [First publication of "Fame is a bee" (J.1763).]
91. "Spring's Orchestra." *Independent*, L (2 June 1898), 1. [First publication of "The saddest noise, the sweetest noise" (J.1764).]
92. "Unpublished Poems by Emily Dickinson." *Atlantic*, CXLIII (Feb., 1929), 180-186. [First publication of J.230, J.341, J.392, J.519, J.569, J.584, J.597, J.607, J.715, J.913. Johnson (Number 47), Appendix 10, incorrectly lists J.1143 as appearing here, and fails to note that J.715 is included.]
93. "New Poems by Emily Dickinson." *SatR*, V (9 March

1929), 751. [Publishes the following poems one week before 1929 edition (Number 34): J.178, J.376, J.413, J.516, J.564, J.627, J.639, J.703.]

94. "New Poems by Emily Dickinson." *NYHTB*, 10 March 1929, p. 4. [First publication of J.253, J.270, J.293, J.464, J.618, J.749, J.907, J.1197. Reprints J.205.]

95. "Unpublished Poems by Emily Dickinson." *Atlantic*, CXLIII (March, 1929), 326-332. [First publication of J.247, J.294, J.344, J.461, J.475, J.616, J.724, J.725, J.734, J.760.]

96. "Twenty New Poems by Emily Dickinson." *LonMerc*, XIX (1929), 337, 350-359. [First publication of J.217, J.243, J.293, J.339, J.453, J.480, J.582, J.610, J.618, J.695, J.721, J.740, J.754, J.913, J.918, J.1053, J.1079, J.1080, J.1092, J.1725.]

97. Barney, Margaret Higginson, and Frederic Ives Carpenter, eds. "Unpublished Poems of Emily Dickinson." *NEQ*, V (1932), 217-220. [Six poems sent to T. W. Higginson, 1860-1875: J.1070, J.1184, J.1257, J.1355, J.1357, J.1359. Reprinted in same year as monograph of same title by Southworth Press, Portland, Maine.]

98. "If I Should be a Queen, by Emily Dickinson." *Atlantic*, CLVI (Nov., 1935), 560. [First publication of "I'm saying every day" (J.373).]

99. "Two Poems by Emily Dickinson." *SatR*, XIII (9 Nov. 1935), 12. [First publication of "A tooth upon our peace" (J.459) and "She staked her feathers, gained an arc" (J.798).]

100. "Glory, by Emily Dickinson." *Atlantic*, CLV (June, 1935), 703. [First publication of "My triumph lasted till the drums" (J.1227).]

101. "Two Unpublished Poems by Emily Dickinson." *YR*, XXV (1935), 76. ["More life went out when he went"

(J.422) and "Somehow myself survived the night" (J.1194).]

102. "An Unpublished Poem by Emily Dickinson." *Cweal*, XXIII, (1935), 124. [First publication of "We grow accustomed to the dark" (J.419).]

103. Bingham, Millicent Todd, ed. "Poems of Emily Dickinson: Hitherto Published Only in Parts." *NEQ*, XX (1947), 3-50. [Fifty-six poems.]

104. Higgins, David J. M., ed. "Twenty-five Poems by Emily Dickinson: Unpublished Variant Versions." *AL*, XXVIII (1966), 1-21. [Supplements T. H. Johnson's variorum edition (Number 47). Variants taken from Millicent Todd Bingham's Dickinson Papers of Amherst and the Library of Congress. Commentary and analysis.]

See also Numbers 59, 105, 138, 211, 296.

b. Prose

105. Higginson, Thomas Wentworth, ed. "Emily Dickinson's Letters." *Atlantic*, LXVIII (1891), 444-456. [Discussion of H's friendship and correspondence with ED. Publishes letters and the following poems: reprint of J.318; first publication of J.299, J.319, J.320, J.323, J.325, J.328, J.365, J.684, J.685, J.816, J.827, J.828, J.1067, J.1365, J.1463, J.1540, J.1561. Reprinted in Higginson's *Carlyle's Laugh and Other Surprises*, pp. 247-283. Boston: Houghton Mifflin Company, 1909; *Jubilee: One Hundred Years of the Atlantic*, pp. 184-199. Edward Weeks and Emily Flint, eds. Boston: Little, Brown and Company, 1957. Partially reprinted in Number 48.]

106. Bianchi, Martha Dickinson, ed. "Selections from the Unpublished Letters of Emily Dickinson to Her Brother's Family." *Atlantic*, CXV (1915), 34-42.

107. "An Emily Dickinson Letter." *MHAQ*, IX (1926), 153-155. [Written to Abiah P. Root, Nov. 6, 1847.]

108. Barney, Margaret Higginson, ed. "Fragments from Emily Dickinson." *Atlantic*, CXXXIX (1927), 799-801. [T. W. Higginson's daughter edits previously unpublished letters from ED to her father.]
109. "Two Unpublished Autograph Letters of Emily Dickinson." *YULG*, VI (1931), 42-43. [To Mrs. Flint.]
110. Birss, John Howard, ed. "A Letter of Emily Dickinson." *N&Q*, CLXIII (1932), 441. [Fragment.]
111. Madigan, Thomas F., ed. *AutA*, I (Dec. 1933), 50. [Partial quotation of letter to Edward Everett Hale, Jan. 13, 1854.]
112. Tyler, Mrs. William, ed. "As I Like It." *Scrib*, XCV (1934), 290. [An ED letter dated Nov. 9, 1877, written to Professor Richard H. Mather.]
113. Allen, Adèle. "The Boltwood House: Memories of Amherst Friends and Neighbors." *AGQ*, XXVI (1937), 297-307. [Contains three previously unpublished notes from ED to Mrs. Boltwood. Reprinted as a monograph of same title in Amherst, Mass., 1937.]
114. Arnold, Hellen H., ed. "'From the Garden We Have Not Seen': New Letters of Emily Dickinson." *NEQ*, XVI (1943), 363-375. [Fourteen letters to Henry Vaughan Emmons written in early 1850's, accompanied by editor's brief discussion of significance. For additional comment see Number 787.]
115. Davidson, Frank, ed. "Some Emily Dickinson Letters." *IQB*, I (1945), 113-118. [Three previously unpublished letters to Mrs. Haven.]
116. Crowell, Annie L., ed. "Emily Dickinson—An Heritage of Friendship." *MHAQ*, XXIX, No. 4 (1946), 129-130. [Reminiscence by daughter of Mary Warner, ED's girlhood friend. Stresses ED's active social life at Mt. Holyoke; denies seclusion was father's wish. Contains two letters and a poem from ED to Mary Warner.]

117. Weber, Carl J., ed. "Two Notes from Emily Dickinson." *CCQ*, XV (1946), 239-240. [To Mrs. Julius H. Seelye.]
118. Bingham, Millicent Todd, ed. "Prose Fragments of Emily Dickinson." *NEQ*, XXVIII (1955), 291-318. [Drafts of miscellaneous notes, letters, poems. Many physically described.]
See also Number 794.

3. Significant Reprints, Chronologically Arranged

119. "The Snake." *SpringR*, 17 Feb. 1866. [Early printing of "A narrow fellow in the grass" (J.986.)]
120. *Critic*, XVII (1890), 305-306. [Brief review of Number 54, reprinting J.67, J.89, J.99, J.182.]
121. "Some Books of Verse." *Overland*, XVII (May, 1891), 550. [Review of Number 54, reprinting J.478, J.712, J.764, J.1078.]
122. "Recent Poetry." *Nation*, LIII (1891), 297. [Review of Number 55, reprinting J.442, J.455, J.1147, J.1393.]
123. "Talk about New Books." *CathW*, LII (1891), 601-603. [Early reprint of J.266, J.318, J.333, J.384, J.712, J.976, J.1052.]
124. *HM*, LXXXII (1891), 318-321. [Reviews Number 55, reprinting J.99, J.187, J.193, J.214, J.241, J.449, J.764, J.1052, J.1078, J.1760.]
125. "Indian Summer." *Dial*, XI (1891), 313. [Early printing of "I died for beauty but was scarce" (J.449).]
126. " 'Letters of Emily Dickinson'." *Critic*, XXVI (1895), 119. [Review of Numbers 52, 53, reprinting "There is no frigate like a book" (J.1263).]
127. "Notes." *Chap-Book*, III (1895), 446. [See Number 26.]
128. "Emily Dickinson's Poems." *LA*, CCII (1896), 479. [Early printing of J.30, J.80, J.908.]
129. *Nation*, LXIII (1896), 275. [Reviews Number 56, reprinting J.31, J.1263, J.1396.]

130. "Ready." *YC*, LXXI (11 Nov. 1897), 568. [Early printing of "They might not need me, yet they might" (J.1391).]
131. *YC*, 18 March 1897. [An early reprint of "Could mortal lip divine" (J.1409).]
132. Brown, Everett Thornton, ed. *Happy Thoughts*. Chicago: The Achmegraph Press, 1912. [Early printing of "They might not need me, yet they might" (J.1391).]
133. ———, ed. *Silver Linings*. Chicago: The Achmegraph Press, 1912. [Early printing of "If I can stop one heart from breaking" (J.919). Reprinted in Brown's *The Spirit of Friendship*. Chicago: The Achmegraph Press, 1913.]
134. "I had not minded walls." *NYHTB*, 10 March 1929, p. 1. [An early printing of J.398.]
135. "Four Poems by Emily Dickinson." *Nation*, CXXVIII (1929), 315. [Reprints J.599, J.970, J.1082, J.1725.]
136. Arnold, Hellen H., ed. *An Emily Dickinson Year Book*. Northampton, Mass.: Hampshire Bookshop, 1948. [A calender with lines by ED alloted to each day. Drawings by Louise B. Graves. Foreword by Arnold stresses normality of ED and family.]
137. Whicher, George F., ed. "Some Uncollected Poems by Emily Dickinson." *AL*, XX (1949), 436-440. [Four poems (J.1391, J.1762, J.1763, J.1764) previously published in periodicals, but excluded from subsequent editions. Speculates on identity of sender, discusses feud over MSS.]
138. Williams, Oscar, ed. "Three Newly-Found Poems." *Mutiny*, XII (1963), 58-59. [Selections from an announced, but not published edition. These "poems" are actually prose fragments arranged in stanzas.]
139. E.E.C. [Coleman, Earl E.], ed. "Emily Dickinson." *PULC*, XXV (1964), 230-231. [Princeton acquires two ED notes

for its manuscript collection. One is to Mrs. James S. Cooper, the other to Mrs. Jonathan L. Jenkins. Both are included in Johnson edition (Number 46).]
See also Number 344.

C. Translations

Czechoslovakian

See Number 2

Dutch

140. Pool, Rosey E., ed. and tr. *Emily Dickinson: Ten Poems.* Amsterdam: A. A. Balkema, 1944.
141. Vestdijk, Simon, ed. *Selected Poems.* Amsterdam: A. A. Balkema, 1940.

French

142. Ansermoz-Dubois, Félix, ed. and tr. *Emily Dickinson: Choix de Poèmes.* Geneva: Editions du Continent, 1945. [English and French versions on opposing pages. Introd. briefly examines previous criticism, gives biographical detail, ED's favorite authors, themes. Several letters translated in introd.]
143. Berger, Claude, and Paul Zweig, trs. *Twenty Poems.* Paris: Lettres Modernes, 1963. [Introd. by Zweig, illustrations by Michèle Katz. English and French.]
144. Bosquet, Alain, tr. *Emily Dickinson.* Paris: Pierre Seghers, 1957. [English and French on opposing pages. Introd. touching on state of American poetry in 1862, ED's childhood, seclusion, posthumous publication, form, style, themes.]

145. Leyris, Pierre, tr. "Poèmes et Lettres d'Emily Dickinson." *Mes*, v, No. 3 (1939), 125-139.
146. Messiaen, P., ed. and tr. *Emily Dickinson: Poèmes Choisis.* Paris: Aubier, 1956.
147. Simon, Jean, tr. *Emily Dickinson: Poèmes.* Paris: Pierre Seghers, 1954. [Reviewed in Number 625.]

German

148. Gruenthal, Lola, ed. and tr. *Emily Dickinson: Gedichte.* Berlin: Henssel, 1959.
149. Hennecke, Hans, ed. and tr. "Emily Dickinson (1830-1886), Gedichte Eingeleitet und Ubertragen von Hans Hennecke." *EurR*, XIII (1937), 297-301.
150. Mathi, Maria, ed. and tr. *Der Engel in Grau: Aus dem Leben und Werk der Amerikanischen Dichterin, Emily Dickinson.* Mannheim: Kessler Verlag, c. 1956. [German translation of poems and letters, with introduction. German and English on opposing pages.]
See also Number 342.

Italian

151. Berti, Luigi, tr. *Sei Poesie di Emily Dickinson.* Rome: Meridiano, 1937.
152. Bini, Martha, tr. *Emily Dickinson: Poesie.* Milan: M. A. Denti, 1946 [?]
153. Coletti, Gladys, ed. and tr. "Scelta di Poesie della Dickinson." *Frontespizio*, No. 4, April, 1937. [Introductory notes. In Italian.]
154. Errante, Guido, ed. and tr. *Emily Dickinson: Poesie.* Milan: Arnoldo Mondadori, 1956. [1956 edition is a single volume, based on Bianchi text; 1959 edition is two volumes, based on Johnson text, with revised preface. Eng-

lish and Italian on opposing pages. Reviewed in Numbers 448 and 463.]

155. Guerrini, Vittoria, ed. and tr. "Tre Poesie di Emilia Dickinson." *MdR*, 7 March 1943. [Translation into Italian, with biographical comment.]

156. Guidacci, Margherita, tr. *Dickinson: Poesie*. Florence: Cya, 1947.

157. ———. *Emily Dickinson: Poesie e Lettere*. Florence: Sansoni, 1961.

158. Izzo, Carlo, tr. *Poesia Americana Contemporanea*. Parma: Guanda, 1949. [Italian translation with prefatory note.]

159. Rebucci, Dyna McArthur, tr. *Emily Dickinson*. Milan: Nuova Accademia, 1961. [Italian translation. Introd. and notes by Sergio Perosa.]

160. Rizzardi, Alfredo. *Lirici Americani*. Caltanissetta, Italy: Sciascia, 1953. [Selected poems translated with preface. In Italian.]

161. Zolla, Elémire, ed. and tr. *E. Dickinson: Selected Poems and Letters*. Milan: Ugo Mursia Editore, 1961.

See also Numbers 9, 176.

Japanese

162. Niikura, Toshikazu, ed. and tr. *Emily Dickinson: A Study and Selected Poems*. Tokyo: Sinozaki Shoten, 1961. [Critical introd. deals with ED's biography, her creative and traditional qualities, her New England literary heritage, her lyric verse, her religious poems, elements of scepticism and mysticism, her relationship to the moderns. Translations based on Todd-Higginson text.]

Polish

163. Ittakowiczówna, I. Kazimiera, ed. *Emily Dickinson: Poezje*. Warsaw: Panstwowy In-t Wydawn, 1965.

Portuguese

164. Krahenbühl, Olívia, tr. *Poesias Escolhidas de Emily Dickinson.* São Paulo: Edição, 1956 [?].

Spanish

165. Domenchina, Juan José, ed. and tr. *Emily Dickinson: Obra Escogida.* S. A. Mexico: Editorial Centauro, 1946.
166. Manent, Mariano, ed. and tr. *Emily Dickinson: Poemas.* Barcelona: Editorial Juventud, S. A., 1957.
167. Pineda, Rafael. "Emily Dickinson." *RNC*, xxv, clvi-clvii (1963), 132-145. [Spanish translations with biographical introd. Brief mention of ED's allusions to South America.]
See also Number 722.

Swedish

168. Blomberg, Erik, and Johannes Edfelt, eds. *Dikter Av Emily Dickinson.* Stockholm: Wahlström and Widstrand, 1949.
See also Number 191.

III. Books about Emily Dickinson

169. Alexander, Charlotte. *The Poetry of Emily Dickinson.* New York: Monarch Press, 1965. [A study guide for undergraduates.]
170. Anderson, Charles R. *Emily Dickinson's Poetry: Stairway of Surprise.* New York: Holt, Rinehart, and Winston, 1960; London: William Heinemann, Ltd., 1960. [Major critical study. Chapters on ED's views on art, nature, self, death and immortality as expressed in her verse. Many excellent explications. Partially reprinted in Numbers 178, 203. Reviewed in Numbers 526, 635, 640, 669, 682, 684.]
171. Bingham, Millicent Todd. *Ancestors' Brocades: The Literary Debut of Emily Dickinson.* New York and London: Harper and Brothers, 1945; N.Y.: Dover, 1967. [Mabel Loomis Todd's daughter recounts problems of editing and publishing. "Creative Editing" contains interesting description of Todd and Higginson's emendations. Biographical data on Dickinson family. See Number 891. Reviewed in Numbers 250, 346, 377, 431, 501, 503, 518, 531, 568, 649, 670, 771, 821, 823, 897, 910, 915.]
172. ———. *Emily Dickinson: A Revelation.* New York: Harper and Brothers, 1954; Toronto: Musson Book Co., Ltd., 1954. [Rumor of ED's love disappointment and subsequent withdrawal was fostered by Sue Dickinson to di-

vert gossip from ED and Judge Lord. Includes ED's letters to Lord.]

173. ———. *Guide to the Use of the Microfilm of Emily Dickinson Manuscripts, Presented by Millicent Todd Bingham to Amherst College, 1956-1957.* Amherst, Mass.: Amherst College, 1957. [See Number 42.]

174. Blake, Caesar R., and Carlton F. Wells, eds. *The Recognition of Emily Dickinson: Selected Criticism since 1890.* Ann Arbor: University of Michigan Press, 1964; Toronto: Ambassador Books, Ltd., 1964; London: Cresset Press, 1964. [An anthology of previously published criticism, chronologically arranged. Discussed in Number 17.]

175. Capps, Jack L. *Emily Dickinson's Reading: 1836-1886.* Cambridge, Mass.: Harvard University Press, 1966; London: Oxford University Press, 1966. [Relies primarily on poetry and letters to reconstruct a list of ED's reading. Chapters on ED's attachment to books, her use of the Bible, her knowledge of British and American authors, her readings in newspapers and magazines. Appendixes include an annotated bibliography of her reading, a list of her Mt. Holyoke texts, a quantitative representation of Biblical allusions. A revision of Number 925.]

176. Cecchi, Emilio, and Giuditta Cecchi, eds. *Emily Dickinson.* Brescia: Morcelliana, 1939. [Critical introd. with selected poems translated into Italian. Reviewed in Numbers 360, 895.]

177. Chase, Richard. *Emily Dickinson.* (American Men of Letters Series.) New York: William Sloane Associates, Inc., 1951; London: Methuen, 1952; Toronto: George J. McLeod, Ltd., 1952; New York: Dell Publishing Company, 1965; Toronto: Saunders, 1965. [An important critical biography analyzing relationship between ED's poetry

and environment. Emphasizes her intellectual development and its effect on her art. Much of her work fails due to American rococo quality, but succeeds when tempered by Puritan severity. Discusses recurring themes and images, aesthetics. Many explications. Reviewed in Numbers 406, 424, 523, 719, 802. Partially reprinted in Numbers 178, 249.]

178. Davis, Thomas M., ed. *Fourteen by Emily Dickinson, with Selected Criticism.* Chicago: Scott, Foresman and Company, 1964. [A casebook. Comments by several critics follow each of fourteen poems. All material previously published. Study questions appended.]

179. Duncan, Douglas. *Emily Dickinson.* (Writers and Critics Series.) Edinburgh: Oliver and Boyd, 1965. [A useful critical introd. dealing with biography, history of publication, aesthetics, literary reputation. Briefly reviews criticism from 1890 to present. Deals with individual poems; extensive explication. Discussed in Number 18.]

180. Fisher, Aileen Lucia, and Olive Rabe. *We Dickinsons: The Life of Emily Dickinson as Seen through the Eyes of Her Brother Austin.* New York: Atheneum Publishers, 1965. [Intended for young readers.]

181. Ford, T. W. *Heaven Beguiles the Tired: Death in the Poetry of Emily Dickinson.* University, Ala.: University of Alabama Press, 1966. [Examines ED's various treatments of death; argues that death is central in her poetry; suggests a relationship to existentialism. Revision of a Univ. of Texas dissertation; see Number 928.]

181a. Franklin, Ralph William. *The Editing of Emily Dickinson.* Madison, Wis.: University of Wisconsin Press, 1967.

182. Gelpi, Albert J. *Emily Dickinson: The Mind of the Poet.* Cambridge, Mass.: Harvard University Press, 1965. [Attempts to join textual analysis with biography. Places ED

in an intellectual and artistic tradition by exploring relationship to Jonathan Edwards, Bryant, Melville, Hawthorne, Poe, Emerson, Thoreau, Whitman, Frost, Stevens, Byron, Keats, Hardy, Henry James, etc. Chapters on ED's preceptors, religion, aesthetics. Revision of a Harvard Univ. dissertation; see Number 930. Discussed in Number 18.]

183. Gould, Jean. *Miss Emily*. Boston: Houghton Mifflin Company, 1946. [A children's book.]

184. Griffith, Clark. *The Long Shadow: Emily Dickinson's Tragic Poetry*. Princeton, N. J.: Princeton University Press, 1964. [A psychoanalytically oriented critical study placing ED in tragic tradition of romanticism. Chapters on child poems, irony, spiritual crisis, time, change, death, love poetry, self, ED's modernity, central symbols in life and poetry. Many extended explications. Chapter V is revision of Number 554. Reviewed in Number 425. Discussed in Number 17.]

185. Hammond, William Gardiner. *Remembrance of Amherst: An Undergraduate's Diary, 1846-1848*. New York: Columbia University Press, 1946. [Describes ED's friends, Amherst as ED must have known it. Introd. by George F. Whicher.]

186. Higgins, David. *Portrait of Emily Dickinson: The Poet and Her Prose*. New Brunswick, N. J.: Rutgers University Press, 1967. [Revision of Number 933. ED's life as revealed through her correspondence. Emotional crisis linked to love for Samuel Bowles.]

187. Jenkins, MacGregor. *Emily Dickinson: Friend and Neighbor*. Boston: Little, Brown and Company, 1930. [Childhood reminiscence. Reviewed in Numbers 345, 456, 851, 878, 909.]

188. Johnson, Thomas H. *Emily Dickinson: An Interpretive*

Biography. Cambridge, Mass.: The Belknap Press of Harvard University Press, 1955; London: Oxford University Press, 1955; Toronto: S. J. Reginald Saunders and Company, Ltd., 1955. [An important critical biography. First part contains chapters on ED's family, friends, cultural legacies; second deals with ED as artist, investigating impact of Newton, Bowles, Wadsworth, Higginson, and Helen Hunt Jackson on life and work. Excellent treatment of ED's prosody, aesthetics, use of Bible, Watt's hymnal. Third part examines themes of nature, death, immortality. Reviewed in Numbers 371, 423, 686, 880, 906, 908. Partially reprinted in Numbers 178, 203, pp. 78-87.]

189. Lalli, Biancamaria Tedeschini. *Emily Dickinson: Prospettive Critiche*. Florence: Le Monnier, 1963. [Discussed in Number 17.]

190. Leyda, Jay. *The Years and Hours of Emily Dickinson*. 2 vols. New Haven: Yale University Press, 1960; Toronto: Burns and MacEachern, Ltd., 1960. [Factual, chronological reconstruction of ED's life. Not intended to be a finished biography, but solid basis for future scholarship. Index. Reviewed in Numbers 359, 508, 589, 684, 833.]

191. Löfmarck, Ellen, ed. and tr. *Emily Dickinson: En Introduktion med Lyriska Tolkningar av Ellen Löfmarck*. Stockholm: Bröderna Lagerström Boktryckare, 1950. [Swedish translation of selected poems with extensive introd.]

192. Longsworth, Polly. *Emily Dickinson: Her Letter to the World*. New York: Thomas Y. Crowell Company, 1965. [Biography, of interest chiefly to young readers.]

193. MacLeish, Archibald, Louise Bogan, and Richard Wilbur. *Emily Dickinson, Three Views: Papers Delivered at Amherst College . . . October 23, 1959*. Amherst, Mass.:

Amherst College Press, 1960. [Fine introd. by Reginald F. French suggests ED's greatness lies not in imagery, prosody, or vocabulary, but in repeated creation of a persona speaking directly to reader in a tone of emotional restraint. For content analysis, see Numbers 221, 275, 329.]

194. McNaughton, Ruth Flanders. *The Imagery of Emily Dickinson.* (University of Nebraska Studies, N.S., No. 4.) Lincoln: University of Nebraska Press, 1949. [Examines sources of ED's imagery—nature, domestic life, religion, law, gems, titles, place names, sense impressions; notes kinds of imagery used in treating nature, death, life, love, immortality.]

195. Patterson, Rebecca. *The Riddle of Emily Dickinson.* Boston: Houghton Mifflin Company, 1951; London: Gollancz, 1953; Toronto: Thomas Allen, 1951. [Expounds theory that Kate Scott Anthon was love object in ED's life and poetry. Reviewed in Numbers 424, 473, 605, 719, 739, 801.]

196. Phi Delta Gamma, Zeta Chapter. [Alma G. Watson, ed.] *Guests in Eden: Emily Dickinson, Martha Dickinson Bianchi.* New York: Zeta Chapter, Phi Delta Gamma, 1946. [A tribute to ED and Mme. Bianchi, consisting of essays and poems on both women. For content analysis, see Numbers 285, 291, 307.]

197. Pickard, John B. *Emily Dickinson: An Introduction and Interpretation.* (American Authors and Critics Series.) New York: Holt, Rinehart and Winston, Inc., 1967. [Written for college students. Provides an excellent biographical and critical introduction to ED, together with a review of scholarship.]

198. Pollitt, Josephine. *Emily Dickinson: The Human Background of Her Poetry.* New York and London: Harper and Brothers, 1930. [An unrealiable biography noted for

its theory that Major Hunt, Helen Hunt Jackson's husband, was ED's love. No discussion of poetry. For corrections, see Numbers 415, 780. Reviewed in Numbers 345, 390, 456, 462, 673, 675, 851, 878.]

199. Porter, David T. *The Art of Emily Dickinson's Early Poetry.* Cambridge, Mass.: Harvard University Press, 1966; London: Oxford University Press, 1966. [Examines poems J.1 through J.298 to trace the artistic development. Deals with prosody, kinetic imagery, personae, hymnal form, irony, theme of aspiration, style. Numerous explications. A revision of Number 940. Reviewed in Number 360.]

200. Powell, Desmond Stevens. *Emily Dickinson.* (Colorado College Publication, Gen. Ser. No. 200.) Colorado Springs: Colorado College, 1934. [Condemns shoddy biography and editing. Discusses versification, love poetry, ED's poetic worth, similarities with Donne. Calls for availability of MSS, new edition.]

201. Power, Sister Mary. *In the Name of the Bee: The Significance of Emily Dickinson.* New York: Sheed and Ward, 1943. [Foreword by Alfred Barrett. History of ED's religious thought, viewing her as a great Catholic poet who chanced to be born Protestant. Reviewed in Numbers 482, 896. For a previously published chapter, see Number 596.]

202. Rosenbaum, S[tanford]. P[atrick]. *A Concordance to the Poems of Emily Dickinson.* Ithaca, N. Y.: Cornell University Press, 1964. [Produced with the aid of a computer. Reviewed in Number 556. Discussed in Number 17. See also Number 770.]

203. Sewall, Richard B., ed. *Emily Dickinson: A Collection of Critical Essays.* Englewood Cliffs, N. J.: Prentice-Hall, Inc., 1963. [Viewing the 1955 publication of Johnson's

text (Number 47) as a literary milestone, Sewall's anthology of previously published criticism focuses on the period following the variorum edition. Sewall's introd. generalizes about criticism of new era, comments on some selections, assesses ED's importance. Reviewed in Number 752. Discussed in Number 16.]

204. Tabb, John Bannister. *John Bannister Tabb on Emily Dickinson.* New York: Spiral Press (Seven Gables Bookshop), 1950. [A separately bound facsimile letter by Tabb, Sept. 20, 1897, expressing appreciation of ED and acknowledging his similarity to her. Brief foreword by T. H. Johnson comparing the two.]

205. Taggard, Genevieve. *The Life and Mind of Emily Dickinson.* New York and London: Alfred A. Knopf, Inc., 1930; Toronto: Ryerson Press, 1934. [An early attempt to trace intellectual development. Little critical comment on poetry or letters. Theorizes that George Gould was object of ED's love. Reviewed in Numbers 345, 446, 456, 462, 485, 675, 776, 851, 876, 878, 909. Partially reprinted in Number 178, pp. 267-270. Factual correction in Number 746.]

206. Thackrey, Donald E. *Emily Dickinson's Approach to Poetry.* (University of Nebraska Studies, N. S. No. 13.) Lincoln: University of Nebraska Press, 1954. [An important study emphasizing ED's attitudes toward language and her relationship to mysticism, viewing her aesthetic as an outgrowth of her notion of language and tendency toward mysticism. Partially reprinted in Numbers 203, pp. 51-69; 178, pp. 35-37.]

207. Tusiani, Giuseppe. *La Poesia Amorosa di Emily Dickinson.* New York: The Venetian Press (Seven Gables Bookshop), 1950. [Study of love poetry. In Italian. For a partial reprint in English, see Number 208.]

208. ———. *Two Critical Essays on Emily Dickinson.* The Venetian Press (Seven Gables Bookshop), 1951. [Essays entitled "The Love Poetry of Emily Dickinson" and "Rhythm and Rhyme in Emily Dickinson's Letters." The former is a partial reprint and translation of Number 207.]

209. Ward, Theodora. *The Capsule of the Mind: Chapters in the Life of Emily Dickinson.* Cambridge, Mass.: The Belknap Press of Harvard University Press, 1961; London: Oxford University Press, 1961. [Treats ED's youth, central crisis in her life (1858-1865), the period after 1865, and her friends: the Joseph Hollands, Samuel Bowles, and T. W. Higginson. Chapters reprinted from Numbers 59, 866, 867, 868. Reviewed in Number 834.]

210. Wells, Henry W. *Introduction to Emily Dickinson.* Chicago: Packard and Company (Hendricks House, Inc.), 1947. [Three part organization: first is biographical, giving data, inferring development of ED's mind, relationship between mind and poetry; second examines environment and sets her into historical context; third is critical. Reviewed in Number 493. Partially reprinted in Numbers 178, pp. 72-75; 203, pp. 45-50.]

211. Whicher, George Frisbie. *This Was a Poet: A Critical Biography of Emily Dickinson.* New York and London: Charles Scribner's Sons, 1938; Philadelphia: Albert Saifer (Dufour Editions), 1952; Ann Arbor: University of Michigan Press, 1957. [An early and still valuable critical biography. ED's youth in Amherst, friends, withdrawal, critics and editors, love poetry, nature poetry. "The Sources of a Style" explores ED's debt to Puritan tradition (use of Bible, hymnal meter, etc.), to American humor traditions, to Emerson and others. See also Number 887. First publication of J.1578. Edition of 1938 reviewed in

Numbers 474, 492, 511, 515, 696, 829, 861. Partially reprinted in Numbers 178, pp. 91-93, 137-138; 203, pp. 41-44; 249, p. 109.]

212. Wood, Clement. *Emily Dickinson: The Volcanic Heart.* n.p. [privately printed], 1945.

See also Numbers 33, 35, 40, 113, 162, 350, 794, 889.

IV. Chapters and Parts of Chapters on Emily Dickinson

213. Allen, Gay Wilson. "Emily Dickinson." *American Prosody*, pp. 307-319. New York: American Book Company, 1935. [Discussion of editions through *Further Poems* (Number 34), ED's metrical regularity, rhyme, relationship to Imagists. Stylistic comparison with Emerson. Reprinted in Number 174, pp. 176-186.]
214. Anon. "Emily Dickinson." *Winkler Prins Algemeene Encyclopaedie*. Amsterdam: N. V. Uitgevers-Maatschappij "Elsevier," 1934.
215. Arnavon, Cyrille. "Redécouverte de l'Amérique: Emily Dickinson." *Histoire Littéraire des Etats-Unis*, p. 355. n.p.: Librairie Hachette, 1953. [Brief, general introd. likening ED to Emerson, Whitman, Metaphysicals, and Imagists.]
216. Auslander, Joseph, and Frank Ernest Hill. "Under Steam and Stone." *The Winged Horse: The Story of the Poets and Their Poetry*, pp. 402-405, 411-412. Garden City, N. Y.: Doubleday, Doran, and Company, 1927. [Contains biographical inaccuracies, brief criticism of work, comparison of ED with Edna St. Vincent Millay.]
217. Bartlett, Phyllis. *Poems in Process*, pp. 84-87. New York: Oxford University Press, 1951. [Brief comment on ED's manner of composition.]
218. Bates, Katharine Lee. *American Literature*, pp. 178-179.

New York: The Macmillan Company, 1898. [Extremely brief and uncritical; ED as gnome of Amherst.]

219. Blair, Walter, *et al.* "Emily Dickinson." *The Literature of the United States*, vol. II, pp. 18-19, 24-25, 176-212. Third edition. Chicago: Scott, Foresman and Company, 1966. [General introduction, explications, ED's use of homely imagery, views on science, religion.]

220. Blankenship, Russell. "Emily Dickinson (1830-1886)." *American Literature as an Expression of the American Mind*, pp. 576-579. New York: Henry Holt and Company, Inc., 1931. [ED's isolation from literary influence.]

221. Bogan, Louise. "A Mystical Poet." In Number 193, pp. 27-34. [A useful examination of ED's relationship to mysticism in general and Blake in particular. Reprinted in Number 203, pp. 137-143.]

222. ———. "The Summers of Hesperides Are Long." *Louise Bogan: Selected Criticism: Prose, Poetry*, pp. 289-294. New York: The Noonday Press, 1955. [Brief survey of biography and early editing. Classifies ED as mystical and metaphysical. Reviewed in Number 51.]

223. Bosquet, Alain. "Les Trois Grandes Figures: Edgar Allen Poe, Walt Whitman, Emily Dickinson." *Anthologie de la Poésie Américaine des Origines à Nos Jours,* pp. 20-21. Paris: Librairie Stock, 1956. [Brief, general discussion of life and mind.]

224. Boynton, Percy H. "Emily Dickinson." *Literature and American Life*, pp. 690-699. Boston: Ginn and Company, 1936. [ED's literary reputation, religion, life, poetic themes, relationship to Emerson, technique.]

225. Bradford, Gamaliel. "Emily Dickinson." *Portraits of American Women*, pp. 227-257. Boston: Houghton Mifflin Company, 1917. [Reprinted in *Atlantic*, CXXIV (1919), 216-226; *Portraits and Personalities*, pp. 189-

212. Mabel A. Bessey, ed. Boston: Houghton Mifflin Company, 1933.]

226. Brenner, Rica. "Emily Dickinson." *Twelve American Poets before 1900*, pp. 267-295. New York: Harcourt, Brace and Company, 1933. [Introductory, biographical and critical.]

227. Bronson, Walter C. "Emily Dickinson." *A Short History of American Literature.* Boston: D. C. Heath and Co., 1900. [Brief appreciative comment.]

228. Brooks, Cleanth, and Robert Penn Warren. *Understanding Poetry*, pp. 469-471. New York: Henry Holt and Company, Inc., 1938. [Explicates "Because I could not stop for death" (J.712) and "After great pain a formal feeling comes (J.341). For comment on the latter, see Number 775. Reprint in Number 178, pp. 49-51.]

229. Brown, John Howard, ed. "Dickinson, Emily Elizabeth." *Lamb's Biographical Dictionary of the United States.* Boston: James H. Lamb, 1900.

230. Cambon, Glauco. "Dickinson: Confrontation of the Self with Otherness in the Inner Space." *The Inclusive Flame: Studies in American Poetry*, pp. 27-49. Bloomington: Indiana University Press, 1963. [Contrasts ED with Whitman and others. Discusses conflict between identity and otherness in life and poetry. Brief treatment of humor, concept of nature, religion. Extended footnote on circumference. From the Italian version published in *Tematica e Sviluppo della Poesie Americana*, pp. 9-80. Rome: Edizioni di Storia e Letteratura, 1956.]

231. ———. "Emily Dickinson and the Crisis of Self-Reliance." *Transcendentalism and Its Legacy*, pp. 123-133. Myron Simon and Thornton H. Parsons, eds. Ann Arbor: Univ. of Michigan Press, 1966. [ED contrasts with Thoreau and Emerson because she often conceives of experience and belief as beset by doubt and fear.]

232. Cestre, Charles. "*La Poésie.*" *La Littérature Américaine*, pp. 189-191. Paris: Librairie Armand Colin, 1945.

233. ———. *Les Poètes Américains*, pp. 91-103. Paris: Les Presses Universitaires de France, 1948. [Considers ED a poet of stature, though faulty in technique. Discusses ED as modern, briefly compares her with Whitman, comments on nature poetry, love poetry, religion, relationship to metaphysical poets. In French.]

234. Clark, Harry Hayden, ed. "Emily Dickinson." *Major American Poets*, pp. 897-902. New York: American Book Company, 1936. [Brief introductory essay comparing ED with Emerson and discussing her aesthetics. Comments on ideas in twenty-eight poems. Bibliography.]

235. Collins, John Churton. *Studies in Poetry and Criticism*, p. 75. London: George Bell and Sons, 1905. [Brief comment associating ED with Emerson.]

236. Daiches, David, and William Charvat, eds. *Poems in English: 1530-1940*, pp. 727-728. New York: The Ronald Press Company, 1950. [A series of brief notes on individual poems.]

237. Donoghue, Denis. "Emily Dickinson." *Connoisseurs of Chaos: Ideas of Order in Modern American Poetry*, pp. 100-128. New York: The Macmillan Company, 1965. [Impressionistic review of ED's faith in imagination, her self-confidence, her intellectual quest, her spirit. Explications.]

238. Duncan, Joseph Ellis. "Emily Dickinson." *The Revival of Metaphysical Poetry: The History of a Style, 1800 to the Present*, pp. 77-88. Minneapolis: University of Minnesota Press, 1959. [General review of ED's techniques: scientific, religious, household imagery, etc. No complete explication. Denies direct influence.]

240. Erskine, John. "Reading and Writing." *The Complete*

Life: A Guide to the Active Enjoyment of the Arts and of Living, p. 50. N. Y.: Messner, 1943. [Denies ED is universal.]

241. Fletcher, Robert S., and Malcolm O. Young. *Amherst College Biographical Record of the Graduates and Non-Graduates, 1821-1921.* Centennial Edition. Amherst, Mass.: Amherst College, 1927.

242. Foerster, Norman. "Later Poets: Emily Dickinson." *The Cambridge History of American Literature*, vol. III, pp. 31-34. W. P. Trent, S. P. Sherman, and C. Van Doren, eds. New York: The Macmillan Company, 1933. [Contains errors of fact and judgment. ED is securely second-rate. Reprinted in Number 174, pp. 94-97.]

243. Friar, Kimon, and John Malcolm Brinnin, eds. "Emily Dickinson." *Modern Poetry: American and British*, pp. 456-457. New York: Appleton - Century - Crofts, Inc., 1951. [Explicates "Wonder is not precisely knowing" (J.1331). For comment on this interpretation, see Number 720.]

244. Frohock, Wilbur Merrill. "Emily Dickinson: God's Little Girl." *Strangers to This Ground: Cultural Diversity in Contemporary American Writing*, pp. 98-110. Dallas, Texas: Southern Methodist University Press, 1961. [Investigates impact of Amherst society on ED's verse, ED's use of personae, especially that of a child.]

245. Frye, Northrop. "Emily Dickinson." *Major Writers of America*, vol. II, pp. 3-16. Perry Miller, ed. New York: Harcourt, Brace and World, Inc., 1962. [Biographical detail, history of publication. Touches on literary reputation, style, grammar and syntax, diction, prosody, prose, religion, treatment of nature, innocence, experience, immortality, death. Reprinted in *Fables of Identity: Studies in Poetic Mythology*, pp. 193-217. New York: Harcourt, Brace and Company, 1963.]

246. Galinsky, Hans. "Wege in die Dichterische Welt Emily Dickinsons." *Geist Einer Freien Gesellschaft*, pp. 221-294. Heidelberg: Quelle and Meyer, 1962.

247. Gohdes, Clarence L. "New Voices in Verse." *Literature of the American People*, pp. 729-736. Arthur H. Quinn, ed. New York: Appleton-Century-Crofts, Inc., 1951. [Biographical detail, history of publication, prosody, imagery, themes.]

248. Gorman, Herbert S. "Emily Dickinson." *The Procession of Masks*, pp. 41-54. Boston: B. J. Brimmer Company, 1923. [ED as spontaneous poet of unpolished technique. Praises nature description, concentrated meanings, apt use of adjectives and verbs. Briefly associates ED with Imagists, Transcendentalism, mysticism.]

249. Gwynn, Frederick Landis, Ralph W. Condee, and Arthur O. Lewis, eds. *The Case for Poetry*, pp. 105-106, 109. New York: Prentice-Hall, Inc., 1954. [Reprinted from Numbers 177, 211, 333, 806, 828. Brief explications of "Because I could not stop for death" (J.712) by Allen Tate, Yvor Winters, and Richard Chase; "Safe in their alabaster chambers" (J.216) by George F. Whicher and Grover Smith.]

250. Hackett, Francis. "Emily Dickinson." *On Judging Books: In General and in Particular*, pp. 226-228. New York: John Day Company, 1947. [Appreciative and uncritical review of Numbers 51, 171. Contains biographical inaccuracies.]

251. Halleck, Reuben Post. "Emily Dickinson, 1830-1886." *The Romance of American Literature*, pp. 257-263. New York: American Book Company, 1934. [Introductory essay commenting on ED's modernity, biography, publication.]

252. Hartley, Marsden. "Emily Dickinson." *Adventures in the*

Arts: Informal Chapters on Painters, Vaudeville, and Poets, pp. 198-206. New York: Boni and Liveright, 1921. [Appreciative, impressionistic, and inclined to see ED's verse as pleasantly light.]

253. Heath, Monroe. *Great American Authors at a Glance.* Menlo Park, Calif.: Pacific Coast Publishers, 1962.

254. Hicks, Granville. "Emily Dickinson." *The Great Tradition*, pp. 124-130. New York: The Macmillan Company, 1933. [Compares ED with her literary contemporaries, finding she excelled them by withdrawing from society and creating a personal, untainted poetry. Severence was a source both of strength and weakness. Reprinted as "Emily Dickinson and the Gilded Age" in Number 174, pp. 167-172.]

255. Higgins, David James Monroe. "Emily Dickinson's Prose." In Number 203, pp. 162-177. [ED as letter-writer: her stylistic development, correspondents, relationship between poetry and prose. Reprinted from Number 933. See also Number 186.]

256. Higginson, Mary Thacher. *Thomas Wentworth Higginson: The Story of His Life*, pp. 312-313, 368-369. Boston: Houghton Mifflin, 1914. [Records Higginson's reaction to ED's death and his deep admiration for her poetry.]

257. Howe, M. A. De Wolfe. "Emily Dickinson: Enigma." *Who Lived Here? A Baker's Dozen of Historic New England Houses and Their Occupants*, pp. 57-68. Boston: Little, Brown and Company, 1952. [Introductory essay, primarily biographical. Photographs by Samuel Chamberlain of ED house in Amherst and ED room in Houghton Library.]

258. Hunt, Percival. "Emily Dickinson." *A Series of Eight Radio Talks on Some Writers of Older New England*, pp.

48-56. Radio Publications, No. 36. Pittsburgh: University of Pittsburgh, 1928. [Biographical and critical. Intended for a non-scholarly audience.]

259. Hurd, Charles, and Eleanor Bronson Hurd, eds. *A Treasury of Great American Letters*, pp. 149-151. New York: Hawthorn Books, Inc., 1961.

260. Jacoby, John E. "L'esthétique de la Sainteté: Emily Dickinson." *Le Mysticisme dans la Pensée Américaine,* pp. 241-276. Paris: Les Presses Universitaires de France, 1931. [Assesses ED's relationship to American mysticism, concluding that hers is a mysticism of nature. Focuses on ED's reaction against Puritanism, her penchant for renunciation, her poetry dealing with death, immortality, nature. In French.]

261. James, Alice. *Alice James: Her Brothers—Her Journal*, pp. 248-249. Anna Robeson Burr, ed. New York: Dodd, Mead and Company, 1934. [An early appreciative opinion of ED's poetry.]

262. Jennings, Elizabeth. "Idea and Expression in Emily Dickinson, Marianne Moore, and Ezra Pound." *American Poetry*, pp. 97-113. (Stratford-Upon-Avon Studies 7.) John Russell Brown, Bernard Harris, and Irvin Ehrenpreis, eds. London: Edward Arnold (Publishers) Ltd., 1965. [All three poets are essentially observers; they share, while using very different techniques, a contemplative attitude toward men and affairs.]

263. Johnson, Thomas H. "Emily Elizabeth Dickinson." *Encyclopaedia Britannica*, vol. VII, pp. 384-385. Chicago: University of Chicago, 1963.

264. Josephson, Matthew. "Those Who Stayed." *Portrait of the Artist as American*, pp. xxii-xxiii, 173-178. New York: Harcourt, Brace and Company, 1930. [Concentrates on ED's seclusion, viewing it as a comment on society.]

265. Kelley, William Valentine. "Emily Dickinson: The Hermit Thrush of Amherst." *Down the Road and Other Essays of Nature, Literature, and Religion*, pp. 214-283. New York: Eaton and Mains, 1911. [An early biographical and critical essay. Discusses ED's relationship to Emily Brontë. Examines ED and love, nature, death, religion.]
266. Kreymborg, Alfred. "The Tippler Leaning against the Sun." *Our Singing Strength: An Outline of American Poetry (1620-1930)*, pp. 193-205. New York: Coward-McCann, Inc., 1929. [Discusses ED as literary, social, and religious rebel. Touches on humor, attitudes toward nature, science. Rates her as best female poet.]
267. Le Breton, Maurice. *Anthologie de la Poésie Américaine Contemporaine*, pp. 35-40, 62-63. Paris: Les Éditions Denoël, 1948. [ED as a modern and forerunner to Imagists. Seclusion helped her develop poetic independence. In French.]
268. Leisy, Ernest Erwin. "Poetry." *American Literature: An Interpretative Survey*, pp. 218-219. New York: Thomas Y. Crowell, 1929. [Brief, appreciative comment. ED anticipated Imagists.]
269. Lewis, R. Roland. *Creative Poetry*, pp. 330-331. Palo Alto, Calif.: Stanford University Press, 1931.
270. Lewisohn, Ludwig. *Expression in America*, pp. 356-363. New York: Harper and Brothers, 1932. [Sketchy discussion of ED as transitional figure. Maintains that ED's psychological verse is unskilled as opposed to her lyrical verse.]
271. Leyda, Jay. "Miss Emily's Maggie." *New World Writing*, pp. 255-267. (Third Mentor Selection.) New York: The New American Library of World Literature, Inc., 1953. [ED household as seen through the letters of domestic servant Margaret Maher. Partially reprinted in Number 190.]

272. Loggins, Vernon. "Unpremeditated Art: Emily Dickinson." *I Hear America*, pp. 9-31. New York: Thomas Y. Crowell, 1937. [Views ED as a modern because verse has air of spontaneity. Touches on life, poetry, literary reputation.]

273. Lowell, Amy. "Emily Dickinson." *Poetry and Poets: Essays by Amy Lowell*, pp. 88-108. Boston: Houghton Mifflin Company, 1930. [Discussion of ED as precursor to Imagists. Malign impact of friends and society inclined her toward neurosis.]

274. ———. *The Works of Stephen Crane*, vol. VI, Introd. Wilson Follett, ed. New York: Alfred A. Knopf, 1925. [Considers ED's impact on Crane.]

275. MacLeish, Archibald. "The Private World." In Number 193, pp. 13-26. [Tone is the source of ED's greatness. This essay is a version of Number 276. Parts of the two are virtually identical; parts are quite different.]

276. ———. "The Private World: Poems of Emily Dickinson." *Poetry and Experience*, pp. 91-114. Boston: Houghton Mifflin Company, 1961; Cambridge, Mass.: The Riverside Press, 1961. [Examines relationship between sound and meaning; emphasis on tone as most important device. Reprinted in Number 203, pp. 150-161.]

277. Martz, Louis L. "Whitman and Dickinson: Two Aspects of the Self." *The Poem of the Mind: Essays on Poetry, English and American*, pp. 82-104. N. Y.: Oxford University Press, 1966. [ED contrasts with Whitman in being minutely analytical and controlled. Examination of love poems, religious poems.]

278. Moore, Virginia. "Emily Dickinson." *Distinguished Women Writers*, pp. 145-160. New York: E. P. Dutton and Company, 1934. [Introductory, biographical.]

279. Muirhead, James Fullarton. "Some Literary Straws." *The*

Land of Contrasts: A Briton's View of His American Kin, pp. 178-186. London and New York: John Lane, 1900. [Finds ED unpolished in technique, but generally worthy.]

280. Nyren, Dorothy, ed. and comp. "Dickinson, Emily." *A Library of Literary Criticism*, pp. 132-136. New York: Frederick Ungar Publishing Company, 1960.

281. Pattee, Fred Lewis. "Emily Dickinson." *A History of American Literature Since 1870*, pp. 340-341. New York: The Century Company, 1915. [Believes Lavinia would have done a service to the world had she burned the poems.]

282. ———. "The Transition Poets." *The New American Literature: 1890-1930*, pp. 196-199. New York: The Century Company, 1930. [A more sympathetic treatment than in Number 281. Deals with both life and work; factual errors in both categories. For corrections, see Number 777.]

283. Pearce, Roy Harvey. "Emily Dickinson." *The Continuity of American Poetry*, pp. 174-191. Princeton, N. J.: Princeton University Press, 1961. [Denies ED is Transcendentalist. Examines culture's influence on ED's style, noting that limitations gave rise to poetry reflecting egocentric world view. Considers egocentric style a nineteenth-century phenomenon enriched by ED. Comparison with Emerson.]

284. Perrine, Laurence. *Sound and Sense: An Introduction to Poetry*, pp. 33, 138-139. New York: Harcourt, Brace, and World, Inc., 1963. [Explicates "There is no frigate like a book" (J.1263) and "Apparently with no surprise" (J.1624).]

285. Pollitt, Josephine. "In Lands I Never Saw." In Number 196, pp. 34-37. [A superficial and often undocumented

survey of ED's popularity in Syria, Czechoslovakia, England, France, Russia, Manila, Spain, Latin America.]

286. Poulet, Georges. "Emily Dickinson." *Studies in Human Time*, pp. 345-350. Elliott Coleman, tr. Baltimore: Johns Hopkins Press, 1956. [ED's poetry rejects past and future joy, accepting only present pain. Hence, suffering unifies past, present, and future, making them the equivalent of eternity. Only death interrupts time's monotony.]

287. Praz, Mario. *Antologia Anglo-Americana.* Milan: Principato, 1936. [In Italian.]

288. Rand, Frank Prentice. "Amherst Authors—Mostly Poets." *The Village of Amherst: A Landmark of Light*, pp. 229-230. Amherst, Mass.: Amherst Historical Society, 1958. [Brief biographical mention.]

289. Reiss, Edmund. "Recent Scholarship on Whitman and Dickinson." *The Teacher and American Literature: Papers Presented at the National Council of Teachers of English*, pp. 115-127. Champaign, Ill.: National Council of Teachers of English, 1965.

290. Roberts, R. Ellis. "Uncut Stones." *Reading for Pleasure and Other Essays*, pp. 185-190. London: Methuen, 1928. [ED is inspired but technically unpolished. Comparison with Mary Coleridge.]

291. Root, E. Merrill. "The Soul Unto Itself." In Number 196, pp. 39-41. [Rhapsodic, diffused claim that ED is valued for her soul rather than poetic craft and that her seclusion permitted a fuller life.]

292. Rourke, Constance. "Round Up." *American Humor: A Study of the National Character*, pp. 266-270. New York: Harcourt, Brace and Company, 1931. [Views ED as comic poet. Discusses use of irony, tragi-comedy, Yankee humor. A thorough study of ED's humor has not yet been done.]

293. Shackford, Martha Hale. "Emily Dickinson: 1830-

1886." *Talks on Ten Poets: Wordsworth to Moody*, pp. 112-120. New York: Bookman Associates, 1958. [Discusses ED as a lyricist whose source of power was her intensity of spiritual experience, her sensitivity to paradox and irony, her courageous acceptance of life.]

294. Southworth, James G[ranville]. "Emily Dickinson." *Some Modern American Poets*, pp. 14-27. New York: The Macmillan Company, 1950; Oxford: Blackwell, 1950. [Considers ED's seclusion, love poems, death poems, domestic imagery, diction, prosody, use of ritual. Finds her intellectually vigorous but too withdrawn from daily life to achieve greatness. Most often her work is immature, sexually frustrated, superficial, redundant, sentimental, trivial, obscure.]

295. Spiller, Robert E. "Art and the Inner Life: Dickinson, James." *The Cycle of American Literature: An Essay in Historical Criticism*, pp. 163-169. New York: The Macmillan Company, 1955. [Brief discussion of ED's place in American Society as defined by her withdrawal from it.]

296. Sweetser, Kate Dickinson. "Emily Dickinson: A Girl of Genius." *Great American Girls*, pp. 105-136. New York: Dodd, Mead and Company, 1931. [Biographical emphasis, concentrating on early years. First publication of "Death's waylaying not the sharpest" (J.1296).]

297. Taggard, Genevieve, ed. "Circumference." *Circumference: Varieties of Metaphysical Verse, 1456-1928*, pp. 3-13. New York: Covici Friede, 1929. [Compares ED with Donne.]

298. Taylor, Walter Fuller, ed. "Emily Dickinson." *A History of American Letters*, pp. 281-282. Boston: American Book Company, 1936. [Brief introductory essay viewing ED in historical context.]

299. Unger, Leonard, and William Van O'Connor, eds. "Em-

ily Dickinson." *Poems for Study: A Critical and Historical Introduction*, pp. 547-548. New York: Holt, Rinehart and Winston, 1964. [Explicates "Because I could not stop for death" (J.712).]

300. Untermeyer, Louis, ed. "Emily Dickinson." *Modern American Poetry*, pp. 7-9, 88-94. New York: Harcourt, Brace and Company, 1950. [Brief comparison with Christina Rossetti. Touches on ED's literary reputation, aesthetics, biography, her editors, critics, biographers. Attempts to evaluate ED's work without dealing with specific poems.]

301. ———. "Emily Dickinson." *Makers of the Modern World*, pp. 132-138. New York: Simon and Schuster, Inc., 1955. [Biographical and critical.]

302. ———. "Emily Dickinson." *A Treasury of Great Poems, English and American*, pp. 943-948. New York: Simon and Schuster, Inc., 1942. [Introductory, biographical. Brief comparison with Christina Rossetti.]

303. ———. "The Religious Conceit: Play for God's Sake." *Play in Poetry*, pp. 48-51. New York: Harcourt, Brace and Company, 1938. [Metaphysical wit in ED's poetic treatment of God.]

304. ———. "The Soul Selects: Emily Dickinson." *Lives of the Poets*, pp. 579-590. New York: Simon and Schuster, Inc., 1959. [Useful introductory essay. Biographical comments more extensive than the critical. Concise history of editing MSS.]

305. Van Doren, Carl. *American Literature: An Introduction*, pp. 67-70. Los Angeles: U. S. Library Association, Inc., 1933. [Brief appreciative note touching on ED's estrangement from social and literary worlds.]

306. Van Doren, Carl, and Mark Van Doren. "Emily Dickinson." *American and British Literature since 1890*, pp. 7-10. New York and London: The Century Company, 1925. [Brief, introductory.]

307. Van Doren, Carl. "Emily Dickinson." *What is American Literature?*, pp. 91-95. New York: William Morrow, 1935. [Brief, general, introduction. Reprinted in Number 54, introd.; Number 196, pp. 42-44.]

308. Van Doren, Mark, ed. *Introduction to Poetry*, pp. 12-16, 39-42. New York: The Dryden Press, Inc., 1951. [Explicates "I had not minded walls" (J.398) and "The soul selects her own society" (J.303). Reprinted in *Enjoying Poetry*, pp. 12-16, 39-42. Mark Van Doren, ed. New York: William Sloane Associates, Inc. 1951; Number 174, pp. 264, 267.]

309. ———. "Nerves Like Tombs." *The Private Reader: Selected Articles and Reviews*, pp. 170-174. New York: Henry Holt and Company, Inc., 1942. [Reviews Numbers 34, 39. ED as poet of wit in metaphysical tradition. An expansion of Number 859.]

310. Van Kranendonk, A. G. *Geschiedenis van de Amerikaanse Literatuur,* pp. 300-305. Amsterdam: N. V. Uitgevers Maatschappi, G. A. Van Oorschot, 1946.

311. Van Loon, Hendrik Willem. "And Now A Rather Strange Combination, Emily Dickinson and Frédéric Chopin, But Emily Has the Time of Her Life, and Chopin Shows Us What Can Be Done with a Minni-piano." *Van Loon's Lives*, pp. 731-766. New York: Simon and Schuster, Inc., 1942. [Whimsical treatment of ED at an imaginary dinner party. Biographical inaccuracies.]

312. Vestdijk, Simon. "Over de Dickteres Emily Dickinson." *Lier en Lancet*, vol. I, pp. 9-51. The Hague: Nijgh and van Ditmar, 1939.

313. Villard, Léonie. "Emily Dickinson." *La Poésie Americaine*, pp. 78-84. Paris: Bordas Frères, 1945. [Discusses relationship between ED's restricted external life and expansive inner life. Briefly treats ED's affinities with Emerson, Blake, Emily Brontë.]

314. Walcutt, Charles Child, and Edwin Whitesell, eds. "Dickinson." *The Explicator Cyclopedia*, vol. I, pp. 55-88. Chicago: Quadrangle Books, 1966. [Reprints selected articles previously published in *Explicator*.]

315. Ward, Alfred Charles. "Emily Dickinson." *American Literature, 1800-1930*, pp. 43-52. New York: The Dial Press, 1932; London: Methuen, 1932. [Discussion of ED's world view, her relation to society, past and present, and her relation to late nineteenth century literature. Brief comparison with Whitman, extended comparison with Housman. Reprinted in Number 174, pp. 145-153.]

316. Weirick, Bruce. "The Period of Reconstruction." *From Whitman to Sandburg in American Poetry: A Critical Survey*, pp. 96-97. New York: The Macmillan Company, 1924. [Brief and superficial.]

317. Welland, Dennis S. R. "Emily Dickinson and Her 'Letter to the World'." *The Great Experiment in American Literature: Six Lectures*, pp. 53-78. Carl Bode, ed. London: Heinemann, Ltd., 1961; New York: Frederick A. Praeger, 1961. [Shyness as characteristic of ED's personality and poetry. Treats relationship between letters and poems, the nature poetry, definition poems, little girl persona, tendency toward sentimentality, Puritan elements, metrics, rhyme.]

318. Wells, Anna Mary. *Dear Preceptor: The Life and Times of Thomas Wentworth Higginson*. Boston: Houghton Mifflin Company, 1963. [Chapters on ED's life, relationship with Higginson, history of editing and publication of MSS. Reviewed in Number 590.]

319. Wells, Henry W. "Emily Elizabeth Dickinson." *Collier's Encyclopedia*, vol. VI, pp. 448-449. New York: P. F. Collier and Son Corp., 1955.

320. ———. "Frugality and Infinity." *The American Way*

of Poetry, pp. 67-77. (Columbia Studies in American Culture No. 13.) New York: Columbia University Press, 1943. [Investigates impact of environment on ED's verse, seeing ED divided between worldliness and mysticism. Valuable comments on ED's religion, nature poetry, domestic imagery, affinities with metaphysical poets, similarities with Emerson.]

321. Wetherell, J. E. "Poems by Emily Dickinson." *Later American Poems*, pp. 185-186. Toronto: Copp, 1896. [Brief introd. to early anthology selection.]

322. Whicher, George F. "Emily Dickinson." *Encyclopaedia of Literature*, vol. II, p. 1084. Joseph T. Shipley, ed. New York: Philosophical Library, 1946.

323. ———. "Emily Elizabeth Dickinson." *Dictionary of American Biography*, vol. V, pp. 297-298. Allen Johnston and Dumas Malone, eds. New York: Charles Scribner's Sons, 1930.

324. ———. "Emily [Elizabeth] Dickinson." *The Oxford Companion to American Literature*, pp. 194-195. Third Edition. James D. Hart, ed. New York: Oxford University Press, 1956.

325. ———. "Emily Dickinson: American Poet." *The Encyclopedia Americana*, vol. IX, pp. 83-84. New York: Americana Corporation, 1956.

326. ———. "Emily Dickinson Among the Victorians." *Poetry and Civilization*, pp. 41-62. Harriet F. Whicher, ed. Ithaca, N. Y.: Cornell University Press, 1955. [Views ED as a modern who escaped fetters of Victorianism. Reprinted in Number 174, pp. 235-250.]

327. ———. "New England Poet." *Mornings at 8:50*, pp. 11-16. Northampton, Mass.: The Hampshire Bookshop, 1950. [Brief, introductory.]

328. ———. "Poetry After the Civil War." *American Writ-*

ers on American Literature, pp. 374-388. John Macy, ed. New York: H. Liveright, Inc., 1931. [ED in context of her Puritan background and in relation to her literary contemporaries. Poetry based on shifting proportions of sensual and psychological experience. ED's isolation saved her from triviality.]

329. Wilbur, Richard. "Sumptuous Destitution." In Number 193, pp. 35-46. [ED transmutes a personal sense of deprivation into poetic theme. Reprinted in Number 203, pp. 127-136; *In Other Words: Amherst in Prose and Verse*, pp. 129-140. Horace W. Hewlett, ed. Amherst, Mass.: Amherst College Press, 1964.]

330. Williams, Stanley T. "Emily Dickinson." *Chambers's Encyclopaedia,* vol. IV, pp. 498-499. New York: Oxford University Press, 1950.

331. ———. "Experiments in Poetry: Sidney Lanier and Emily Dickinson." *Literary History of the United States*, vol. I, pp. 899-916. 3rd revised edition. Robert E. Spiller, *et al.*, eds. New York: The Macmillan Company, 1963. [Biographical detail with attention to ED's ties with society and culture. Exploration of intellectual and artistic development. Reprinted in Number 174, pp. 251-260.]

332. Wilson, Rufus Rockwell. *New England in Letters*, pp. 304-305. New York: A. Wessels Company, 1904. [Brief appreciative comment.]

333. Winters, Yvor. "Emily Dickinson and the Limits of Judgment." *Maule's Curse: Seven Studies in the History of American Obscurantism*, pp. 149-168. Norfolk, Conn.: New Directions, 1938. [Classifies ED's poems by subject-matter, explicating representative selections. Highly personal evaluations. Reprinted in Winters' *In Defense of Reason*, pp. 283-299. New York: Swallow Press, 1947; Numbers 174, pp. 187-200; 203, pp. 28-40. Partially re-

printed in Numbers 178, pp. 31-34, 86, 104-105, 119-120; 249, p. 105.]

334. Witham, W. Tasker. "Emily Dickinson." *Panorama of American Literature*, pp. 145-150. New York: Stephen Daye, Inc., 1947.

335. Wood, Clement. "Emily Dickinson: The Shrinking Seer." *Poets of America*, pp. 82-96. New York: E. P. Dutton and Company, 1925. [Impressionistic discussion of biography and poetry. ED as mystic.]

V. Articles and Parts of Articles on Emily Dickinson

336. Abbott, Lawrence F. "Emily Dickinson." *Outl*, CXL (1925), 211-213. [A former Amherst undergraduate (1877-1881) makes appreciative remarks on ED.]
337. Abenius, Margit. "Emily Dickinson." *BLM*, III (Sept., 1934), 18-23.
338. Adair, Virginia H. "Dickinson's 'One Day Is There of the Series'." *AN&Q*, V (Nov., 1966), 35. [Takes exception to Number 905.]
339. Adams, M. Ray. *NEQ*, XXXII (1959), 555-558. [Reviews Number 50, finding fault with most aspects of Reeves' editing.]
340. Adams, Richard P. "Dickinson Concrete." *ESQ*, No. 44 (1966), 31-35. [ED's poems describe the concrete actualities of life.]
341. ———. "Pure Poetry: Emily Dickinson." *TSE*, VII (1957), 133-152. [Maintains ED's poetry is pure by virtue of its concreteness. Applies methods of new criticism. Considers other critics' approaches and estimations.]
342. A. E., and U. von G. "Emily Dickinson." *DW*, 12 June 1898, p. 13; 19 June 1898, p. 1. [Essay and translations in German.]
343. Agrawal, Ishwar Nath. "Emily Dickinson: A Study of Diction." *LCM*, V (1962), 95-100.
344. Aïdé, Hamilton. "Poems by Emily Dickinson." *NC*, XXXI

(1892), 703-706. [Reviews Number 54, concluding ED's careless technique mitigated somewhat by her strength of imagination. Reprints J.136, J.193, J.333, J.712.]

345. Aiken, Conrad. "The Dickinson Myth." *YR*, XX (1930), 393-396. [Reviews Numbers 187, 198, 205. Dismisses Pollitt and Taggard as conjectural.]

346. ———. "The Dickinson Scandal." *NR*, CXIII (1945), 25-26. [Review of Numbers 51, 171. Amusing account of personal interview with Bianchi; speculates concerning still unpublished poems; evaluation of present collection.

347. ———. "Emily Dickinson." *Dial*, LXXVI (1924), 301-308. [Biographical data. Relates ED to Transcendentalists. Touches on her religion, nature poetry, treatment of metaphysical questions, epigrammatic style, death poetry, prosody. Reprinted in *Reviewer's ABC: Collected Criticism of Conrad Aiken from 1916 to the Present*, pp. 156-163. Rufus A. Blanshard, ed. New York: Meridian Books, Inc., 1935; *Bookman,* LXVII (1924), 8-12; Numbers 28, introd.; 174, pp. 110-117; 203, pp. 9-15.]

348. ———. "Emily Dickinson and Her Editors." *YR*, XVIII (1929), 796-798. [Reviews Number 34, praising poems, but condemning editing.]

349. Aldrich, Thomas Bailey. "In Re Emily Dickinson." *Atlantic*, LXIX (1892), 143-144. [Review of Number 54. Condescending praise overpowered by Aldrich's condemnation of ED's grammar, rhyme, meter. Charges lack of thought, coherence, form. In its time, an influential essay. Reprinted in Numbers 174, pp. 54-56; 178, pp. 11-13; Aldrich's *Ponkapog Papers*, pp. 107-111. Boston: Houghton Mifflin Company, 1903, retitled as "Un Poète *Manqué*"—a revised version.]

350. Allen, Adèle. "The First President's House: A Reminiscence." *AGQ*, XXVI (1937), 93-104. [Childhood memo-

ries of Miss Emily after her seclusion began. Emphasis on her garden, her father, brother. Reprinted as a monograph of same title in Amherst, Mass., 1937.]

351. Allen, Caroline C. "The Homestead in Amherst." *HornBk*, XXXIII (Feb., 1957), 30-34. [Personal reminiscence by a woman whose family received cakes and notes from ED.]

352. Alling, Kenneth Slade. "Declaration." *Measure*, No. 22 (Dec., 1922), pp. 15-16.

353. Anderson, Charles R. "The Conscious Self in Emily Dickinson's Poetry." *AL*, XXXI (1959), 290-308. [ED's verse as a potential poetry of ideas. Examination of major themes: truth, balance between heart and mind, personal essence.]

354. ———. "Dickinson's 'Reverse Cannot Befall'." *Expl*, XVIII (1960), Item 46. [Reprinted in Number 314.]

355. ———. "From a Window in Amherst: Emily Dickinson Looks at the American Scene." *NEQ*, XXXI (1958), 147-171. [ED as social critic.]

356. ———. "The Trap of Time in Emily Dickinson's Poetry." *ELH*, XXVI (1959), 402-424. [ED believed man's mind was incarcerated in time, preventing it from comprehending truth, beauty, nature—all timeless. Poetry offered liberty, immortality.]

357. ———. *AL*, XXX (1958), 371-376. [Reviews Number 46. Commends Johnson's editing, making two minor corrections. Examines letters, noting stylistic maturation coincident with poetic outburst of 1858. Particularly admires vol. II, partly for ED's ideas on poetic theory and technique.]

358. ———. *MLN*, LXXI (1956), 386-390. [Very favorable review of Number 47.]

359. ———. *MLN*, LXXVI (1961), 904-907. [Review of Number 190.]

360. ———. *NEQ*, XXXIX (1966), 522-528. [Review of Numbers 176, 199, 794.]
361. Anderson, John Q. "The Funeral Procession in Dickinson's Poetry." *ESQ*, No. 44 (1966), 8-12. [Explicates several ED funeral poems.]
362. Anderson, Paul W. "The Metaphysical Mirth of Emily Dickinson." *GaR*, XX (1966), 72-83. [The spirit of ED's poetry is both comic and metaphysical, a fact that has major consequences for her aesthetic. Numerous explications.]
363. Andó, Midori. "On Death in the Poems of Emily Dickinson." *Gak*, No. 276 (Dec., 1962), pp. 56-66.
364. ———. "A View of Nature in Emily Dickinson's Poems." *Gak*, No. 280 (April, 1963), pp. 63-76.
365. Angoff, Charles. "Emily Dickinson and Religious Poetry." *Tomorrow*, VII (1947), 24. [Classifies ED as religious poet but does not elaborate.]
366. Anon. "Book Reviews." *AW*, XXXVIII (May, 1924), 28-30. [Review of Number 35.]
367. Anon. "Emily Dickinson." *SpringR*, 1 Feb., 1925.
368. Anon. "The Emily Dickinson Centenary." *CurL*, No. 266 (1931), pp. 42-43.
369. Anon. "Emily Dickinson and Some Early Critics." *SpringR*, 3 Aug. 1930, p. 5E.
370. Anon. [O'Connor, William Van.] "Emily Dickinson: The Domestication of Terror." *TLS*, 9 Sept. 1955, p. 532. [Touches on biography, editing, historical position. Reprinted in O'Connor's *The Grotesque: An American Genre and Other Essays*, pp. 98-108. Carbondale: Southern Illinois University Press, 1962.]
371. Anon. "Emily Dickinson: The Making of an American Poet." *TLS*, 13 Jan. 1956, pp. 13-15. [Reviews Numbers 47, 188, minimizing the errors in Bianchi-Hampson text

(Number 37), but nevertheless applauding Johnson's labors. Finds little new in Johnson's biography.]

372. Anon. "Emily Dickinson: New England Poet, Recluse Because She Didn't Like Own Appearance." *BosP*, 2 March 1930.

373. Anon. "The Emily Dickinson Papers." *AAN*, X (Oct., 1957), 2-4.

374. Anon. "Emily Dickinson Papers Are Given to Harvard." *PW*, CLVII (1950), 2456.

375. Anon. "The Emily Dickinson Room." *HLB*, V (1951), 386-387. [Describes room in Harvard's Houghton Library which contains MSS and memorabilia.]

376. Anon. "Emily Dickinson's Year at Mount Holyoke Seminary." *SpringR*, 10 Nov. 1929, p. 5E.

377. Anon. "Memories of Emily." *Time*, XLV (16 April 1945), 100-104. [Appreciative review of Numbers 51, 171.]

378. Anon. "Miss Dickinson's Poetry." *Critic*, XX (1892), 61. [Ridicules ED's technique.]

379. Anon. "Miss Emily Dickinson of Amherst." *SpringR*, 18 May 1886, p. 4; *AmhR*, 19 May 1886, p. 4. [Obituary. Reprinted in Number 35, pp. 103-105 where Bianchi attributes the authorship to Sue Dickinson.]

380. Anon. "Mystical Poet Whose Ideas Were Heretical." *SpringR*, 26 Oct. 1924.

381. Anon. "New Names for the Hall of Fame?" *PW*, CXVII (1930), 1334-1335. [Speculates that ED may be elected to Hall of Fame.]

382. Anon. "The Newest Poet." *LonDN*, 2 Jan. 1891. [Reviews Number 54, attacking ED's rhymes, grammar, logic. Reprinted in Number 174, pp. 24-27.]

383. Anon. "A Northern Poet and a Southern One." *UNCEB*, II (Sept., 1932), 27-29. [Pedagogical approach to ED and Lizette Woodworth Reese.]

384. Anon. "Our Poetical New England Nun." *LD*, LXXXII (2 Aug. 1924), 34. [Discusses briefly various critics' opinions of ED's poetry: Conrad Aiken, Thomas Bailey Aldrich, Allen Nevins.]

385. Anon. "A Poet." *SRP*, LXXII (5 Sept. 1891), 279. [Reviews Number 54. Admires poems though finds them technically faulty. Reprinted in Number 174, pp. 38-41.]

386. Anon. "The Point of View." *Scrib*, IX (1891), 395-396. [Regrets ED's lack of form. Reprinted as "Form and Substance," Number 174, pp. 34-36.]

387. Anon. "Recent American Poetry." *Nation*, LX (1895), 402. [ED briefly compared with John B. Tabb.]

388. Anon. "Recent Poetry: Emily Dickinson." *Critic*, XVI (1891), 346. [Reviews Number 55, finding ED's work formless. For a reply, see Number 818. Reprinted in Number 174, pp. 50-51.]

389. Anon. "Second Series of the *Poems by Emily Dickinson*." *ChiTrib*, 12 Dec. 1891. [Discusses ED's childlike qualities; excuses her imperfections in form because they emanate from the same source as her genius. Reviews Number 55. Reprinted in Number 174, pp. 45-49.]

390. Anon. "The Week's Reading." *Outl*, CLIV (1930), 309-311. [Review of Number 198. Favorable.]

391. Anon. "What the Critics Say About Emily Dickinson's Poems." *AmhR*, 3 Dec. 1890.

392. Anon. *DUJ*, IX (Dec., 1947), 29-31. [Reviews Numbers 37, 51.]

393. Anthony, Mother Mary. "Emily Dickinson's Scriptural Echoes." *MR*, II (1961), 557-561. [Explores New Testament allusions in "There came a day at summer's full" (J.322). Reprinted in Number 178, pp. 45-48.]

394. Arms, George, *et al*. "Dickinson's 'A Bird Came Down the Walk'." *Expl*, II (1944), Item 61. [Reprinted in Number 178, pp. 2-3.]

395. ———. "Dickinson's 'There's a Certain Slant of Light'." *Expl*, II (1944), Item 29.

396. ———, *et al.* "Dickinson's 'These Are the Days When Birds Come Back'." *Expl*, II (1944), Item 29. [Reprinted in Numbers 178, pp. 2-3; 314, pp. 80-81.]

397. Armstrong, Martin. "The Poetry of Emily Dickinson." *Spec*, CXXX (6 Jan. 1923), 22-23. [An appreciative, somewhat diffused biographical and critical essay. Reprinted in Number 174, pp. 105-109.]

398. Arvin, Newton. *AL*, XXVIII (1956), 232-236. [Appreciative review of Number 47. Proposes readers' edition based on Johnson text.]

399. Avery, Christine. "Science, Technology, and Emily Dickinson." *BBAAS*, No. 8 (1964), pp. 47-55. [ED's attitude is ambivalent.]

400. Baldi, Sergio. "Appunti per uno Studio sulle Poesia della Dickinson." *Let*, VI (1942), 76-88.

401. ———. "La Poesia di Emily Dickinson." *SA*, II (1956), 45-66. [Meaning in ED's poetry derives from her concept of life as consisting of three stages: love, death, immortality. First stage, the wifely state is most common in ED's poetry. In it she looks toward immortality. Her vocabulary involves imagery of reality and escape. The technical means by which ED reconciles this condition of conflict is what relates her to the metaphysical poets. Reprinted in English in *SR*, LXVIII (1960), 438-449.]

402. Baldini, Gabriele. "Tre Secoli di Poesia Americana." *NA*, LXXXII (1947), 392-394.

403. Baldwin, Eleanor. "Emily Dickinson." *Palenque*, IV (1931), 32-33.

404. Banzer, Judith. "'Compound Manner': Emily Dickinson and the Metaphysical Poets." *AL*, XXXII (1961), 417-433. [Argues for direct influence, listing possible sources for ED's acquaintance with metaphysical verse.]

405. Barbot, Mary Elizabeth. "Emily Dickinson's Parallels." *NEQ*, XIV (1941), 689-696. [Finds parallel passages for several ED poems in works of Rev. Wadsworth and T. W. Higginson.]
406. Barrett, William. "Death and the Maiden." *PR*, XIX (1952), 364-367. [Reviews Number 177, finding Chase's approach to ED is logical when it should be emotional.]
407. Bartlett, Alice Hunt. "Dynamics of American Poetry." *PoR*, XXXVIII (1947), 289. [Compares ED with Melville Cane.]
408. Bass, Althea. "A Classmate of Emily Dickinson." *Colop*, V (1934), Pt. 19, Item 8. [Quotes from essays by Sarah Worcester, ED's classmate at Mount Holyoke. Conventionality of writing and thought indicates the school norm against which ED was bound to revolt.]
409. Bassi, Emma. "Emily Dickinson." *AION-SG*, III (1960), 271-282.
410. Bates, Arlo. "Miss Dickinson's Poems." *BosC*, 23 Nov. 1890. [Reviews Number 54, finding ED's work technically flawed, but inspired. Reprinted in Number 174, pp. 12-18.]
411. Bates, Katharine Lee. "A House of Rose." *YR*, XIV (1925), 396-399. [Review of Numbers 32, 35. Sympathetic treatment of ED as hot house plant. Regrets Bianchi's omissions in collection of letters.]
412. Beck, Warren. "Poetry's Chronic Disease." *EJ*, XXXIII (1944), 362-363. [Explicates "Go not too near a house of rose" (J.1434).]
413. Benét, Stephen Vincent. "The Book of the Month." *Bookman*, LIX (1924), 732-735. [Reviews Number 35, warmly praising both ED and her biographer.]
414. Benét, William Rose. "Round About Parnassus." *SatR*, VI (30 Nov. 1929), 488. [Comments on Joseph Auslan-

der's "Letter to Emily Dickinson" in *Letters to Women*, finding it a critical as well as poetic achievement. Briefly compares ED with Amy Lowell.]

415. Bennett, Mary A. "A Note on Josephine Pollitt's *Emily Dickinson: The Human Background of Her Poetry.*" *AL*, II (1930), 283-286. [Corrects biographical data in Number 198.]

416. Berenson, Adrienne. "Emily Dickinson's Social Attitudes: A Dissenting View." *WHR*, VI (1952), 351-362. [Social and religious protest seen in ED's life and poetry.]

417. Bianchi, Martha Dickinson. "Emily Dickinson." *SatR*, I (2 Aug. 1924), 20. [Bianchi defends herself against charge of suppressing biographical data.]

418. ———. "Letter from Madame Bianchi." *SCM*, II, No. 2 (1941), 2, 26. [A sketchy mention of ED's friendship with two Smith College faculty members, Clark Seelye and Mary Jordan.]

419. Bingham, Millicent Todd. "Emily Dickinson's Earliest Friend." *AL*, VI (1934), 191-192. [Reply to Whicher's Number 889. Newton was not mentioned in Number 53 because nothing could be discovered about him.]

420. ———. "Emily Dickinson's Handwriting: A Master Key." *NEQ*, XXII (1949), 229-234. [Bingham does not supply the key, but points out the possibility of dating MSS through ED's handwriting.]

421. Birdsall, Virginia O. "Emily Dickinson's Intruder in the Soul." *AL*, XXXVII (1965), 54-64. [Examines group of poems having in common preoccupation with knowledge, an anticipated visit, household imagery. Discussed in Number 18.]

422. Blackmur, Richard P. "Emily Dickinson: Notes on Prejudice and Fact." *SoR*, III (1937), 323-347. [Discusses various critical approaches to ED. Puts forth own, i.e., that her

greatness is found in ability to combine words. Finds bulk of her poetry fails through lack of form and control. Those poems which succeed reveal a sense of crisis, an aptitude for language, a personal vision. Reprinted in Blackmur's *The Expense of Greatness*, pp. 106-138. New York: Arrow Editions, 1940; *American Harvest*, pp. 229-256. Allen Tate and John Peale Bishop, eds. New York: L. B. Fischer Company, 1942; Blackmur's *Language as Gesture*, pp. 25-50. New York: Harcourt, Brace and Company, 1952; Number 174, pp. 201-223.]

423. ———. "Emily Dickinson's Notation." *KR*, XVIII (1956), 224-237. [Review of Numbers 47, 188. Discusses problem of making a readers' edition of ED with regularized punctuation, but with faithful rendering of thought which preceded the word. Johnson's biography sheds some light on the thought and consequently may illuminate the word. Blackmur views ED as a nuptial poet, comparable to Herrick and Rilke. Compares also with Gide regarding sense of guilt, principle, egoism, temperament. Remarks on syntax. Reprinted in Number 203, pp. 78-87.]

424. ———. "A Plea for the Essay." *KR*, XIV (1952), 530-534. [Review of Numbers 177, 195. ED as emotionally unstrung New England eccentric. Chase and Patterson should have confined efforts to essays.]

425. Blake, Caesar R. *NEQ*, XXXVII (1964), 552-554. [Generally favorable review of Number 184.]

426. Bloom, Margaret. "Emily Dickinson and Dr. Holland." *UCC*, XXXV (1933), 96-103. [Biographical data on Holland, his literary reputation, religious verse, novels, friendship with ED, impact of religious views on ED.]

427. Blunden, Edmund. "Nineteenth Century Poetry." *N&A*, XLVIII (1931), 574. [ED is in tradition of Victorian women poets with mystical inclinations.]

428. ———. "An Unguessed Poetry." *N&A*, XLVI (1930), 863. [A favorable review of Numbers 32, 34, viewing ED as a lyricist. Reprinted in Number 174, pp. 134-137.]

429. Bocquet, Leon. "La Littérature Américaine." *NRCrit*, XV (1931), 162.

430. Bogan, Louise. "The Poet Dickinson." *Poetry*, XLVIII (1936), 162-166. [Review of Number 39, pointing out need for definitive edition and trustworthy biography in order to reveal artistic and intellectual development.]

431. ———. "Verse." *NY*, XXI (21 April 1945), 84-86. [Review of Numbers 51, 171. History of feud over MSS. ED's unnatural relationship with father made her forever childlike, though artistically mature.]

432. Bolin, Donald W. "Dickinson's 'A Clock Stopped'." *Expl*, XXII (1963), Item 27.

433. ———. "Emily Dickinson and the Particular Object." *Forum*, III, xi (1962), 28-31. [Compares ED's approach to nature with that of Emerson, Thoreau. Deals with themes of time, death, winged animals. Explications.]

434. Bond, C. C. J. "Haunting Echo." *CanL*, XVI (1963), 83-84.

435. Bravo Villasante, Carmen. "Carta sobre los Epistolarios Femeninos." *Asomante*, XV (1959), 7-19. [Brief mention of ED as letter-writer. In Spanish.]

436. ———. "Las Escritoras Norteamericanas." *Asomante*, XVIII (1962), 31-48.

437. ———. "Las Escritoras Clásicas Norteamericanas." *CHA*, LXVI (1966), 205-222.

438. Breed, Paul F. " 'Boanerges' a Horse?" *AN&Q*, I (1963), 86. [Query concerning J.585. For replies, see Numbers 451, 641.]

439. Brégy, Katherine. "Emily Dickinson: A New England Anchoress." *CathW*, CXX (1924), 344-354. [Reviews

Numbers 32, 35. Primarily biographical. Brief consideration of ED and mysticism.]

440. Brigdman, Richard. "Emily Dickinson: A Winter Poet in a Spring Land." *MSpr*, LVI (1962), 1-8. [Review of recent ED scholarship followed by brief discussion of imagery, tone, syntax, theme of death. In English.]

441. Brooks, Van Wyck. "Emily Dickinson." *Schol*, XXXVIII (10 March 1941), 17-19, 22. [Introductory, primarily biographical. Reprinted in Brooks's *New England: Indian Summer*, pp. 316-329. New York: E. P. Dutton and Company, 1940; *American Authors Today*, pp. 241-252. Whit Burnett and Charles Eli Slatkin, eds. Boston: Ginn and Company, Inc., 1947; Brooks's *A Chilmark Miscellany*, pp. 219-231. New York: E. P. Dutton and Company, 1948.]

442. Brown, Rollo Walter. "A Sublimated Puritan." *SatR*, V (6 Oct. 1928), 186-187. [An early and somewhat outdated treatment. Reprinted in Brown's *Lonely Americans*, pp. 233-257. New York: Coward-McCann, Inc., 1929.]

443. Brunel, Pierre. "Le Corbeau (à Propos de la Transposition par Claudel d'un Poème d'Emily Dickinson)." *RLM*, No. 134-136 (1966), 113-118. [Paul Claudel's translation of "Water is taught by thirst" (J.135) becomes a different poem or a variation on a theme.]

444. Bulgheroni, Marisa. "L'Eterno Giardino di Emily." *SA*, VIII (1962), 77-92.

445. Burgess, John W. "How I Found Amherst College and What I Found, Including Reminescences of Emily, Lavinia, Susan Gilbert, and Austin Dickinson." *AAQ*, Nov., 1927.

446. Burton, Richard. "Discussion of Genevieve Taggard's *The Life and Mind of Emily Dickinson*." *CR*, V (1930), 445-452. [Reviews Number 205.]

447. Cambon, Glauco. "L'Edizione Critica di Emily Dickinson." *Aut Aut*, XXXII (1956), 155-164. [Reviews Number 47.]

448. ———. "On Translating Dickinson." *Chel*, VII (1960), 77-87. [Generally favorable review of Number 154. Problems of translation.]

449. ———. "Violence and Abstraction in Emily Dickinson (1958)." *SR*, LXVIII (1960), 450-464. [ED anticipates Mallarmé, Valéry, Rilke.]

450. Campbell, Harry Modean. "Dickinson's 'The Last Night That She Lived'." *Expl*, VIII (1950), Item 54. [Reprinted in Number 314, pp. 70-71.]

451. Capps, Major Jack L. "Dickinson's 'Boanerges'." *AN&Q*, II (1963), 57-58. [A reply to Number 438 concerning J.585.]

452. Carlson, Eric W. "Dickinson's 'I Started Early—Took My Dog'." *Expl*, XX (1962), Item 72. [Reprinted in Numbers 178, pp. 89-90; 314, pp. 69-70.]

453. Carmen, William Bliss. "A Note on Emily Dickinson." *BET*, 21 Nov. 1896. [Reviews Number 56, touching on ED's life, religion, view of nature. Her poetry is second-rate because lacking in sensuousness. Approves of inexact rhymes. Reprinted in Number 174, pp. 61-68.]

454. Carpenter, Frederic I. "Dickinson's 'Farther in Summer Than the Birds'." *Expl*, VIII (1950), Item 33. [Reprinted in Numbers 178, pp. 120-121; 314, pp. 59-60.]

455. ———. "Emily Dickinson and the Rhymes of Dream." *UKCR*, XX, (1953), 113-120. [ED's work is poetic attempt to accommodate reality and dream. Analysis of irregular rhyme as a device for reflecting the difficulty of accommodation. Reprinted in Number 178, pp. 58-59.]

456. ———. *NEQ*, III (1930), 753-757. [Reviews Numbers 187, 198, 205; attention focused on books, not directly on ED.]

457. Carson, Mother Angela. "Dickinson's 'Safe in Their Alabaster Chambers'." *Expl*, XVII (1959), Item 62. [Reprinted in Numbers 178; 314, p. 77.]
458. Case, Josephine Young. *NEQ*, XXIV (1951), 546-548. [Appreciative review of Numbers 53 (1931 edition) and 59.]
459. Catel, Jean. "Emily Dickinson: Essai d'Analyse Psychologique." *RA*, II (1925), 394-405. [ED's father complex. Brief comparison with Charlotte Brontë.]
460. ———. "Emily Dickinson: L'Œuvre." *RA*, III (1925), 105-120. [Appreciative, with much quotation but no explication. Notes an emphasis on escape and childishness. Links briefly with ED's father complex mentioned in Number 459.]
461. ———. "Poésie Moderne aux États-Unis." *RCC* (1933), pp. 210-223; (1933), pp. 345-356. [Considers ED and Whitman within general theory of American literature. Finds the two exemplify America's break from Europe. Primarily biographical.]
462. ———. "Sur Emily Dickinson: À Propos de Deux Livres." *RA*, XIII (1935), 140-144. [Appreciative review of Numbers 198, 205.]
463. Cecchetti, Giovanni. *CL*, X (1958), 73-77. [Reviews Number 154. In Italian.]
464. Cecchi, Emilio. "Emily Dickinson." *CdS*, LXI (1936), 3.
465. Chadwick, Helen Cary. "Emily Dickinson: A Study." *Person*, X (1929), 256-269. [ED as standard-bearer of individual dignity. Touches on biography, religion, letter-writing.]
466. Chase, Richard. "A Poet's Economy." *HopR*, V (1951), 34-37. [What Rourke (Number 292) regards as humor, Chase considers American rococo. Attempts to set straight view of ED as Ariel of Amherst.]

467. Chelifer [Rupert Hughes]. "The Ideas of Emily Dickinson." *GLB*, CXXXIII (1896), 541-543. [Reviews Number 56.]

468. Childs, Herbert E. "Emily Dickinson and Sir Thomas Browne." *AL*, XXII (1951), 455-465. [Compares them in terms of wit, humor, diction, fondness for paradox, ideas on Platonism, religion, immortality. Quotes parallel passages. Concludes influence cannot be proved without more biographical data.]

469. ———. "Emily Dickinson: Spinster." *WHR*, III (1949), 303-309. [ED did not marry because (1) she and her father were shy, (2) her wit frightened men, and (3) she loved Wadsworth.]

470. Chmaj, Betty E. "The Metaphors of Resurrection." *Universitas*, II (1964), 91-109. [Brief allusion to ED's view of salvation.]

471. Christie, John A. "A New Chapter in American Literature." *VAM*, XLII, No. 1 (1956), pp. 2-6, 10.

472. Ciardi, John. "Dickinson's 'I Heard a Fly Buzz'." *Expl*, XIV (1956), Item 22. [Reprinted in Numbers 178, pp. 67-68; 314, pp. 65-66.]

473. ———. *NEQ*, XXV (1952), 93-98. [Humorous review of Number 195, refuting Miss Patterson's thesis.]

474. Clark, Harry Hayden. "Three Spokesmen of Nineteenth Century America." *YR*, XXVIII (1939), 633-637. [Generally appreciative review of Number 211. Criticizes Whicher's dismissal of ED's lover as fictive.]

474a. Clendenning, John. "Cummings, Comedy, and Criticism." *ColQ*, XII (1963), 48-49. [E.E. Cummings and ED both use surprise as an aspect of style, a technique typical of American humorists.]

475. Clough, Wilson O. "Dickinson's 'When I Hoped I Feared'." *Expl*, X (1951), Item 10. [Reprinted in Number 314, pp. 86-87.]

476. C. M. E. "Letters to the Editors." *Critic*, XX (Feb., 1892), 105. [Brief mention.]

477. Comings, Lois Leighton. "Emily Dickinson." *MHAQ*, VIII (1924), 133-139.

478. Connelly, James T. "Dickinson's 'I Heard a Fly Buzz When I Died'." *Expl*, XXV (1966), Item 34.

479. ———. "Dickinson's 'Wild Nights'." *Expl*, XXV (1967), Item 44.

480. Connely, Willard. "Emily Dickinson in Her Life, Letters, and Poetry." *Essays by Divers Hands*, Vol. XXIII, pp. 1-19. Harold Nicolson, ed. London: Oxford University Press, 1947. [Largely biographical, with emphasis on men influencing ED's life. Brief mention of Shakespeare's influence.]

481. Connors, Donald F. "The Significance of Emily Dickinson." *CE*, III (1942), 624-633. [An appreciative, but unscholarly discussion of ED's life, nature poetry, love poetry, views on immortality.]

482. ———. *Thought*, XIX (1944), 544-546. [Reviews Number 201, objecting to several important points, but praising chapter on nature poetry.]

483. Coursen, Herbert R., Jr. "Nature's Center." *CE*, XXIV (1963), 467-469. [Melville, Henry Adams, ED break with Emersonian view of nature, point toward new era by considering nature hostile to man.]

484. Craig, G. Armour. *ASc*, XXVII (1958), 518-520. [Favorable review of Number 46.]

485. Crowell, Annie L. "Where Loveliness Keeps House." *MHAQ*, XVII (1931), 239-241. [Reviews Number 205.]

486. Cunliffe, Marcus. *RES*, XII (1961), 434-436. [Review of Number 46.]

487. Curran, George. "Emily Dickinson and Religion." *SCM*, II (Nov., 1941), 7-9. [Analysis of poetry and letters to

determine ED's attitude toward God, the Bible, and immortality.]

488. Curtis, Jared R. "Edward Taylor and Emily Dickinson: Voices and Visions." *SUS*, VII (1964), 159-167. [Both poets were Puritans, secluded, partook of the Baroque tradition by juxtaposition of opposites, wrote terse, irregular verse. Discussed in Number 18.]

489. Cutler, Bruce. "An American Heart of Darkness." *Poetry*, CVI (1965), 401-403. [Brief mention of ED as American metaphysical poet.]

490. D'Agostino, Nemi. "Poe, Whitman, Dickinson." *Belfagor*, VIII (1953), 517-538.

491. Dailey, Mary Ann. "The Locomotive as Visualized by Walt Whitman and Emily Dickinson." *Lit*, No. 6 (1965), pp. 23-25. [Whitman's train is masculine; ED's is feminine (J.585).]

492. Daly, James. "Little Plain Woman with Two Smooth Bands of Redish Hair." *Poetry*, LIII (1939), 312-320. [Reviews Number 211, commending treatment of ED's loves, life in Amherst, seclusion, views on publication, etc.]

493. Dauner, Louise. *NEQ*, XXI (1948), 267-270. [Generally unfavorable review of Number 210.]

494. D'Avanzo, Mario L. " 'Came a Wind Like a Bugle': Dickinson's Poetic Apocalypse." *Ren*, XVII (1964), 29-31. [Discussed in Number 17.]

494a. ———. "Emily Dickinson's Dying Eye." *Ren*, XIX (1967), 110-111.

495. Davidson, Frank. "A Note on Emily Dickinson's Use of Shakespeare." *NEQ*, XVIII (1945), 407-408. ["Tunis," in "A route of evanescence" (J.1463) is derived from *The Tempest*.]

496. ———. " 'This Consciousness': Emerson and Dickin-

son." *ESQ*, No. 44 (1966), 2-7. [Reviews scholarship and suggests many echoes of Emerson in ED's poetry.]

497. Davidson, James. "Emily Dickinson and Isaac Watts." *BPLQ*, VI (1954), 141-149. [ED compared with the hymnodist in terms of form, content, style.]

498. Davis, Lloyd M. "Dickinson's 'I Taste a Liquor Never Brewed'." *Expl*, XXIII (1965), Item 53.

499. Dawson, W. J. "American Books That Have Moved Me." *CCW*, 4 Dec. 1909, pp. 779-780.

500. Delgado-Arias, D. Eugene. "Emily Dickinson: Espiritu Esotérico." *Bitacora*, II (1943), 25-36.

501. Deutsch, Babette. "Miracle and Mystery." *Poetry*, LXVI (1945), 274-280. [Reviews Numbers 51, 171. Biographical puzzles remain despite Mrs. Bingham's labors.]

502. ———. "A Sojourn in Infinity." *Bookman*, LXIX (1929) 303-306. [Review of Number 34. Touches on biography. Judges poetry to be lacking in technique but rich in inspiration.]

503. De Voto, Bernard. "The Easy Chair." *HM*, CXC (1945), 602-605. [Reviews Number 171. Emphasizes hatred and neurosis in ED household. Love poetry was written to the God who failed. For a reply see Number 891.]

504. Dole, Nathan Haskell. "Emily Dickinson's Personality." *BookB*, IX (1892), 157-158. [Recounts a lecture by M. L. Todd on ED's seclusion, church attendance, relations with father. Reprinted in Number 205, pp. 375-377.]

505. Dominicis, Annamaria de. "Della Poetica di E. Dickinson." *Itinerari*, Oct., 1954. [Critical. In Italian.]

506. Dorinson, Zahava Karl. "'I Taste a Liquor Never Brewed': A Problem in Editing." *AL*, XXXV (1963), 363-365. [Examines variants to determine best text.]

507. Douglas, Wallace W. *EAA* (Northwestern University), No. 4, pp. 1-3. [Explication of "I taste a liquor never brewed" (J.214).]

508. Du Pont, M. M. "The Endless Study." *NR*, CXLIII (28 Nov. 1960), 30-32. [Generally appreciative review of Numbers 44, 190. Criticizes Leyda for frequent ellipses, denies that Wadsworth was recipient of "Master" letters, etc.]

509. Earle, Genevieve B. "Some Watchers of the Skies." *BCP*, III (1939), 11-12.

510. Eby, Cecil D. " 'I Taste a Liquor Never Brewed': A Variant Reading." *AL*, XXXVI (1965), 516-518. [Argues that speaker is not poet, but the hummingbird. Hence, poem (J.214) is not unsuccessful self-revelation, but witty treatment of nature. Discussed in Number 18.]

511. Edfelt, Johannes. "Detta Var en Poet." *Strövtåg* (1941), pp. 85-93. [Reviews Number 211.]

512. Elias, Robert H., and Helen L. Elias. "Dickinson's 'Farther in Summer Than the Birds'." *Expl*, XI (1952), Item 5. [Reprinted in Numbers 178, pp. 125-126; 314, pp. 60-61.]

513. Eliot, Mrs. T. A. "Why Was She a Recluse?" *SO*, 19 March 1899. [Two former Amherst residents recount their childhood memories of ED and her family. Reprinted in Numbers 35, Appendix V; 177, pp. 372-375.]

514. Elliott, G. R. *AL*, I (1930), 439-442. [Reviews Number 34, giving brief, generally favorable appraisal of poetry.]

515. Ellis, Milton. *NEQ*, XII (1939), 604-608. [Generally favorable review of Number 211.]

516. Emblen, D. L. "A Comment on 'Structural Patterns in the Poetry of Emily Dickinson'." *AL*, XXXVII (1965), 64-65. [Attacks S. M. Wilson's discussion of structure in ED's poetry (Number 912), pointing out that all poetry and prose uses three part organization: statement, elaboration, conclusion. Discussed in Number 18.]

517. England, Martha Winburn. "Emily Dickinson and Isaac

Watts: Puritan Hymnodists." *BNYPL*, LXIX (1965), 83-116. [Interesting and thorough treatment. ED's reaction to Watts was often that of parodist. Discussed in Number 18. Reprinted in *Hymns Unbidden: Donne, Herbert, Blake, Emily Dickinson and the Hymnographers*, pp. 113-148. N.Y.: New York Public Library, 1966.]

518. Erskine, John. "The Dickinson Saga." *YR*, XXXV (1945), 74-83. [Reviews Numbers 51, 171. Traces the Todd-Bingham-Bianchi struggle over editing of MSS; first-hand anecdotes by Erskine. Reprinted as "The Dickinson Feud" in *The Memory of Certain Persons*, pp. 128-138. Philadelphia: J. B. Lippincott Company, 1947.]

519. Essig, Erhardt H. "Dickinson's 'One Dignity Delays for All'." *Expl*, XXIII (1964), Item 16. [Discussed in Number 17.]

520. Everett, Barbara. *CritQ*, I (1959), 159-162. [Reviews Number 50, briefly comparing ED with Robert Graves in terms of wit and relationship to audience.]

521. Fain, John Tyree. " 'New Poems' of Emily Dickinson." *MLN*, LXVIII (1953), 112-113. [Comments on the number of letters which metrically resemble poems.]

522. Faris, Paul. "Dickinson's 'The Soul Selects Her Own Society'." *Expl*, XXV (1967), Item 65.

522a. ——. "Eroticism in Emily Dickinson's 'Wild Nights!'." *NEQ*, XL (1967), 269-274. [Contrary to the usual interpretation, J.249 is a poem about despair, not sexual fulfillment.]

523. Farrelly, John. "Emily Dickinson." *Scr*, XIX (1952), 76-78. [Reviews Number 177, considering it an inferior treatment of a minor poet.]

524. Fasel, Ida. " 'Called Back': A Note on Emily Dickinson." *IEY*, No. 8 (1963), p. 73.

525. ———. "Emily Dickinson's Walden." *IEY*, No. 7

(1962), pp. 22-28. [Compares ED and Thoreau in terms of withdrawal from society, reactions to Whitman, religion. ED was unconsciously influenced by Thoreau. Discussion of religious poetry, death poetry, use of boy persona.]

526. Feidelson, Charles. *MLN*, LXXVI (1961), 908-910. [Review of Number 170.]

527. Feuillerat, Albert. "La Vie Secrète d'Une Puritaine: Emily Dickinson." *RDM*, XL (1927), 668-691. [Reviews Numbers 32, 35.]

528. Ffrench, Yvonne. "Chronicles: Poetry." *LonMerc*, XXIX (1933), 161-163. [Generally favorable review of Number 32.]

529. Figueira, Gastón. "Emily Dickinson y el Brasil." *Torre*, X (1962), 121-125.

530. Finch, John. "Poet of the Thing Missed." *SCM*, II (Nov., 1941), 10, 27. [Briefly discusses theme of deprivation.]

531. Fletcher, John Gould. "The Ablative Estate." *SR*, LIII (1945), 661-670. [Favorable review of Numbers 51, 171.]

532. Fletcher, William I. "The Amherst Dickinsons and the College." *AGQ*, VI (1917), 179-185.

533. Flores, Kate. "Dickinson's 'I Started Early Took My Dog'." *Expl*, IX (1951), Item 47. [Reprinted in Numbers 178, pp. 87-88; 314, pp. 68-69.]

534. Fodaski, Martha. "Dickinson's ''Twas Like a Maelstrom'." *Expl*, XIX (1961), Item 24. [Reprinted in Number 314, pp. 85-89.]

535. Ford, Thomas W. "Emily Dickinson and the Civil War." *UKCR*, XXXI (1965), 199-203. [War had significant impact on poetry by heightening ED's awareness of death. Work increases in quantity and improves in quality. Four war poems analyzed. Discussed in Number 18.]

536. ———. "Emily Dickinson and Death." *MQ*, IV (1962), 33-44. [Maintains ED's view of death was linked to religion. Traces impact of Puritanism, Transcendentalism, Civil War. Finds techniques—imagery, meter, rhyme, punctuation, syntax—adapted to express her concepts of death. For a book-length version see Number 181.]

537. Frank, Joseph. "Emily Dickinson (1830-1886)." *Prisma*, VI (1947), 21-23.

538. Friedrich, Gerhard. "Dickinson's 'I Heard a Fly Buzz When I Died'." *Expl*, XIII (1955), Item 35. [Reprinted in Numbers 178, pp. 65-67; 314, p. 65.]

539. Frost, Lesley. "La Poesía Norteamericana Moderna." *Insula*, No. 19 (July 1947), p. 2. [Brief comment on ED's aesthetics. In Spanish.]

540. Funato, Hideo. "On Emily Dickinson." *Kam*, No. 5 (1962), pp. 38-49.

541. Gardner, Maude. "Two Famous Girls of Amherst, Mass." *AveM*, XXXVI (1932), 561-563. [ED and Helen Hunt Jackson.]

542. Garlington, Jack. "Emily Dickinson's Curious Biographers." *ColQ*, VI (1957), 170-177. [Traces history and evaluates theories concerning ED's "lover."]

543. Garrow, A. Scott. "A Note on Manzanilla." *AL*, XXXV (1963), 366. [Refutes Johnson's note (Number 47) describing manzanilla as a Cuban port in J.214. It was probably a wine-producing town in southwest Spain. For additional comment, see Number 510, pp. 517, fn. 6. Discussed in Number 16.]

544. Glenn, Eunice. "Emily Dickinson's Poetry: A Revaluation." *SR*, LI (1943), 574-588. [Opposes over-emphasis of biographical criticism which is merely admiring or which selects a single line for approval or contempt. Focuses on poems themselves, giving extensive explication

of five. Concludes ED is a metaphysical rather than a romantic poet. Partially reprinted in Number 178, pp. 107-109.]

545. Goffin, Robert. "Emily Dickinson." *NHQ*, v, xv (1964), 181-186. [ED's aesthetics anticipate those of Mallarmé. Comparison with Nerval and Rimbaud. Discussion of sexual elements in religious poetry. In English. Discussed in Number 17.]

546. Goldsmith, Joseph Hannele. "Inspired, Half-Educated, Puritan, and Feminine." *PR*, XII (1945), 402-404. [Review of Number 51. Focuses solely on ED, condemning rhymes and puns. Finds ED's strengths and weaknesses common to many American writers who are obsessed, reclusive, fascinated with renunciation, badly educated, and too trusting of inspiration.]

547. Gorlier, Claudio. "Proposte per una Lettura di Emily Dickinson." *Aut Aut*, I (1951), 344-347.

548. Grattan, C. Hartley. "Wanted: Unemployed Writers to Study American Literary Problems." *Bookman*, LXXIII (1931), 48-55. [Brief reminder to scholars that mystery of ED's biography is still unsolved.]

549. Graves, Gertrude Montague. "A Cousin's Memories of Emily Dickinson." *BSG*, 12 Jan. 1930, p. 41. [A personal reminiscence.]

550. Graves, Louise B. "The Likeness of Emily Dickinson." *HLB*, I (1947), 248-251. [Relates history of how the ED dagerreotype went through several stages of alteration for the various editions.]

551. Green, Clara Bellinger. "A Reminiscence of Emily Dickinson." *Bookman*, LX (1924), 291-293. [Recounts a childhood meeting with ED, and reviews Number 35.]

552. Greever, Garland. *Person*, XXXVII (1956), 421-424. [Favorable review of Number 40.]

553. Gregory, Horace. "The Real Emily Dickinson." *Cweal*, LXVIII (1958), 449-450. [Commentary on Number 46. Cautions against taking emotional tone of ED's letters too literally.]

554. Griffith, Clark. "Emily Dickinson and *Him*: A Modern Approach to Emily Dickinson's Love Poetry." *IEY*, No. 6 (1961), pp. 13-22. [A revision of Number 555. For a more recent and comprehensive version see Number 184, pp. 149-184.]

555. ———. "Emily Dickinson's Love Poetry." *UKCR*, XXVII (1960), 93-100. [Divides love poetry into three categories: those influenced by contemporary sentimental literature, those based on terror of change, those expressing intense fear of masculinity. Partially reprinted in Number 178, pp. 44-45.]

556. ———. *NEQ*, XXXVIII (1965), 405-407. [Reviews Number 202.]

557. Hampson, Alfred Leete. "Emily Dickinson: Evidence of the Authenticity of Her 'Further Poems'." *BET*, 3 Aug. 1929, p. 3. [Denies editorial tampering. Comments on reception of new edition (Number 34).]

558. Hansen, Waldemar. "Land Ho! Infinity!: Emily Dickinson as a Protestant Telescope." *Horizon*, XVII (1948), 71-76. [Reviews Numbers 37, 51.]

559. Haraszti, Zoltan. "An Emily Dickinson Collection." *BET*, 8 Dec. 1923, p. 6. [Discusses Higginson's collection of ED letters and poems on exhibit in Boston Public Library. Suggests handwriting could help in dating items.]

560. Hartley, Marsden. "Emily Dickinson." *Dial*, LXV (1918), 95-97. [Impressionistic, appreciative.]

561. Herbert, T. Walter. "Near-rimes and Paraphones." *SR*, XLV (1937), 446-449. [Classifies near-rimes, finding twelve basic types.]

562. Herrero Esteban, Jacinto. "Emily Dickinson y Pablo Antonio Cuadra: Proximidad de dos Poemas." *CHA*, LXI (1965), 152-155. [Compares Cuadra's "Interioridad de Dos Estrellas que Arden" with "I died for beauty but was scarce" (J.449). In Spanish.]
563. Herring, Emily Louise. "Domestic Imagery in the Poetry of Emily Dickinson." Wake Forest College, 1962. [An M.A. thesis containing useful tabulation of images.]
564. Hiatt, David. "Dickinson's 'Of Bronze and Blaze'." *Expl*, XXI (1962), Item 6.
565. Higgins, David James Monroe. "In Praise of Emily." *SatR*, XXXVI (30 May 1953), 21. [ED did not lack craft. Answers Number 599.]
566. Higginson, T. W. "Letter to a Young Contributor." *Atlantic*, IX (1862), 401-411. [The essay which encouraged ED to seek Higginson's advice concerning her poems. Reprinted in *Atlantic Essays by Thomas Wentworth Higginson*, pp. 70-92. Boston: James R. Osgood and Company, 1871; Number 751.]
For another article by T. W. Higginson, see Number 105.
567. Hillyer, Robert. "Emily Dickinson." *Fre*, VI (1922), 129-131. [Notes a shift in quality of ED criticism. Turn of century critics, even those who admired her, found her eccentric, whimsical. Critics now are turning to her work with a new seriousness. Hillyer examines ED's style, use of locale, views on religion, death, immortality, war. Reprinted in Number 174, pp. 98-104.]
568. ———. "Emily Dickinson's Unpublished Poems—and Their Genesis." *NYTBR*, 15 April 1945, pp. 3, 20, 22, 24. [Reviews Numbers 51, 171. Applauds Bingham's editing, finding selection best yet published. Touches on ED's meter, rhyme, mystical and metaphysical qualities.]
569. ———. "The Later Emily Dickinson." *HH*, II (1929),

423-425. [Reviews Number 34. Remarks on ED's modernity, speculates on reason poems were witheld from publication, adversely criticizes Bianchi and Hampson's editing.]

570. Hindus, Milton. "Emily's Prose: A Note." *KR*, II (1940), 88-91. [Aspects of ED's poetic style appear in her prose and debase it.]

571. Hinshaw, Edna Bangs. "Some Early Recollections of Emily Dickinson." *BH*, 18 Dec. 1927, sup. p. 3. [Personal reminiscence.]

572. Hirsch, David. "Emily Dickinson's 'Presentiment'." *AN&Q*, I (1962), 36-37. [A plausible reading of J.764. See also Numbers 574 and 738.]

573. ———. "Emily Dickinson's 'Presentiment' Again." *AN&Q*, III (1965), 119-120. [A Reply to Number 738.]

574. ———. "Reply." *AN&Q*, III (1965), 119-120. [Brief response to Number 738 dealing with connotation in "Presentiment is that long shadow on the lawn" (J.764). See also Hirsch's Numbers 572, 573.]

575. H.M. [Harrict Monroe]. *Poetry*, V (1914), 138-140. [Review of Number 38. Brief discussion of ED as Imagist.]

576. Hoepfner, Theodore C. "Because I Could Not Stop for Death." *AL*, XXIX (1957), 96. [Takes exception with aspect of Chase's reading (Number 177) of J.712. Reprinted in Number 178, p. 113.]

577. Hoffman, Frederick J. "The Technological Fallacy in Contemporary Poetry: Hart Crane and MacKnight Black." *AL*, XXI (1949), 97. [Explicates "I like to see it lap the miles" (J.585) in footnote. Reprinted in *Poetry as Experience*, p. 460. Norman C. Stageberg and Wallace Anderson, eds. New York: American Book Company, 1952.]

578. Hogue, Caroline. "Dickinson's 'I Heard a Fly Buzz When I Died'." *Expl*, XX (1961), Item 26. [Reprinted in Numbers 178, pp. 68-69; 314, p. 66.]

579. ———. "Dickinson's 'There Came a Day at Summer's Full'." *Expl*, XI (1952), Item 17. [Reprinted in Numbers 178, pp. 42-44; 314, pp. 78-79.]

580. ———. "Dickinson's 'When I Hoped I Feared'." *Expl*, X (1952), Item 49. [Reprinted in Number 314, pp. 87-88.]

581. Hollahan, Eugene. "Dickinson's 'I Heard a Fly Buzz When I Died'." *Expl*, XXV (1966), Item 6.

582. Howard, Mabel, William Howard, and Emily Harvey. "Dickinson's 'My Wheel Is in the Dark!'." *Expl*, XVII (1958), Item 12. [Reprinted in Number 314, pp. 72-73.]

583. Howard, William. "Dickinson's 'I Can Wade Grief'." *Expl*, XIV (1955), Item 17. [Reprinted in Number 314, p. 64.]

584. ———. "Dickinson's 'I Never Saw a Moor'." *Expl*, XXI (1962), Item 13.

585. ———. "Dickinson's 'Safe in Their Alabaster Chambers'." *Expl*, XVII (1959), Item 62. [Reprinted in Numbers 178, pp. 23-24; 314, pp. 76-77.]

586. ———. "Dickinson's 'There Came a Day at Summer's Full'." *Expl*, XII (1954), Item 41. [Reprinted in Numbers 178, pp. 43-44; 314, pp. 79-80.]

587. ———. "Emily Dickinson's Poetic Vocabulary." *PMLA*, LXXII (1957), 225-248. [Isolates unusual words, explodes theories about ED's favorite words, compares ED's vocabulary to representative English poets of last five centuries. Based on concordance study.]

588. Howells, William Dean. "The Strange *Poems of Emily Dickinson*." *HM*, LXXXII (1891), 318-321. [An early admirer of ED, Howells arrives at the same conclusions re-

garding ED's seclusion, view of fame, technical abilities that today's critics are beginning to accept. Brief comparison with Emerson, Blake, Heine, only to reassert her uniqueness. Reprinted in Numbers 174, pp. 18-24; 178, pp. 9-11.]

589. Howes, Barbara. "Emily, Day by Day." *VQR*, XXXVII (1961), 286-290. [Reviews Number 190.]

590. Huggins, Nathan Irvin. *NEQ*, XXVI (1963), 520-522. [Generally favorable review of Number 318. Focuses on Higginson rather than ED.]

591. Humphries, Rolfe. "Too Difficult a Grace." *NR*, LIX (22 May 1929), 38-40. [Review of Number 34, taking exception with introd., aspects of editing. Brief history of publication.]

592. Hurd, Pearl Strachan. "All the Difference." *CSM*, 15 May 1956, p. 10. [Brief appreciative comment. Recounts interview with Mme. Bianchi.]

593. Ives, Ella Gilbert. "Emily Dickinson: Her Poetry, Prose, and Personality." *BET*, 5 Oct. 1907. [Impressionistic biography and criticism. Rhapsodically appreciative. Reprinted in Number 174, pp. 71-78.]

594. Iwayama, Tajiro. "On the Importance of the Variant Readings of Emily Dickinson's Poems—An Attitude toward the Johnson Version." *SEL*, XLII (1966), 193-207. [In Japanese. Discusses Number 47.]

595. ———. "Process of Transition of Emily Dickinson's Idea: From Death to Immortality." *SH*, No. 64 (March, 1963), pp. 1-26.

596. James [Power], Sister Mary. "Emily's Neighborhood." *CathW*, CLVIII (1943), 143-149. [ED's views on friendship. Reprinted as part of Number 201.]

597. Jenkins, MacGregor. "A Child's Recollection of Emily Dickinson." *ChrU*, XLIV (1891), 776-777. [Personal reminiscence. For book-length version, see Number 187.]

598. Jennings, Elizabeth. "Emily Dickinson and the Poetry of the Inner Life." *REL*, III (1962), 78-87. [ED as lyric poet.]

599. Johnson, Burges. "Inspired and Uninspired Writers." *SatR*, XXXVI (25 April 1953), 45. [ED is inspired but lacking in technique. For a rebuttal, see Number 565.]

600. Johnson, Thomas H. "Dickinson's 'Immured in Heaven'." *Expl*, XI (1953), Item 36. [Reprinted in Number 314, p. 70.]

601. ———. "Emily Dickinson: Creating the Poems." *HLB*, VII (1953), 257-270. [Description of MSS and examination of several worksheets as a key to ED's methods of revising.]

602. ———. "Emily Dickinson: The Prisms of a Poet." *SatR*, XXXIII (3 June 1950), 16-17. [Suggests what may be learned of ED's life and art now that MSS are located at Harvard. Reprinted in Number 174, pp. 261-264.]

603. ———. "Establishing a Text: The Emily Dickinson Papers." *SB*, V (1952-53), 21-32. [Commentary on the primary difficulties in editing MSS. Focuses on variant readings and chronology. Extensive discussion of handwriting, etc.]

604. ———. "The Great Love in the Life of Emily Dickinson." *AH*, VI (1955), 52-55. [Considers what impact ED's love for Wadsworth had on her poetry.]

605. Joost, Nicholas. "The Pain That Emily Knew." *Poetry*, LXXX (1952), 242-245. [Reviews Number 195, praising the effort but condemning the product.]

606. Jordan, Mary Augusta. "Emily Dickinson's Letters." *Nation*, LIX (1894), 446-447. [An early, wise assessment of ED's letters. Discusses stylistic development, relationship between prose and poetry, ED as revealed through her letters. Reprinted in Number 174, pp. 57-61.]

607. Jordan, Raymond J. "Dickinson's 'The Bustle in the House'." *Expl*, XXII (1963), Item 49.
608. Juvonen, Helvi. "Emily Dickinson." *Parn*, VII (1958), 245-249.
609. Kato, Kikuo. "On the Death-Poems of Emily Dickinson." *BTGU*, XIV (1963), 7-10.
610. Kazin, Alfred. "Called Back." *Griffin*, IX, xi (1960), 2-9. [Reviews Number 44. Reprinted in Kazin's *Contemporaries*, pp. 50-56. Boston: Little, Brown and Company, 1962.]
611. Keleher, Julia. "The Enigma of Emily Dickinson." *NMQ*, II (1932), 326-332. [ED's love poetry is more easily explained as part of mystical tradition than as a recounting of an actual love affair.]
612. Kenny, Virginia. "Was Emily Dickinson 'Short of Hearing?' " [*sic*]. *Highl*, XXXIX (1960), 5, 11, 15. [Probably.]
613. Kerman, Joseph. "American Music: The Columbia Series (II)." *HudR*, XIV (1961), 408-418. [Evaluates Aaron Copland's song cycle, *Twelve Poems by Emily Dickinson.*]
614. Keys, F. V. "The Poet in Time and Space." *NAR*, CCXIX (1924), 905-912. [Views ED as tragic victim of environment.]
615. Kerby, J. P. "Dickinson's 'A Bird Came Down the Walk'." *Expl*, II (1944), Item 61. [Reprinted in Number 314, p. 57.]
616. Klett, Ada M. "Doom and Fortitude: A Study of Poetic Metaphor in Annette von Droste-Hulshoff (1797-1848) and Emily Dickinson (1830-1886)." *Monatshefte*, XXXVII (1945), 37-54. [Comparison on basis of personal and artistic qualities. Annette von Droste-Hulshoff is poet of doom; ED is poet of fortitude. In English.]
617. Koopman, Harry Lyman. "Emily Dickinson." *BM*, VIII (1896), 82-92.

618. Kurth, Paula. "Emily Dickinson in Her Letters." *Thought*, IV (1929), 430-439. [Reviews Number 35. Largely biographical comments gleaned from letters or other standard sources.]

619. Lair, Robert L. "Dickinson's 'As by the Dead We Love to Sit'." *Expl*, XXV (1967), Item 58.

620. Lalli, Biancamaria Tedeschini. "Dio Como Ansia." *SA*, VIII (1962), 71-76.

621. ———. "Sul Vocabolario Poetico di Emily Dickinson." *SA*, X (1964), 181-200. [Discussed in Number 18.]

622. Lang, Andrew. "A Patriotic Critic." *ILN*, C (1892), 14-15. [A now-famous attack on ED's grammar.]

623. ———. "Some American Poets." *ILN*, XCVIII (1891), 307. [Review of Number 54. Charges bad rhyme, grammar, logic. Reprinted in Number 174, pp. 36-38.]

624. Larrabee, Ankey. "Three Studies in Modern Poetry: The Use of Death and Puritan Theology in Emily Dickinson's Poetry, the Symbol of the Sea in Crane's 'Voyages,' Prufrock and Joseph Wood Krutch." *Accent*, III (1943), 115-121. [Takes issue with Tate (Number 828) regarding ED's use of Puritan theology. Finds ED's view of redemption, immortality, even death itself is personal rather than doctrinal. Partially reprinted in Number 178.]

625. Las Vergnas, Raymond. "Lettres Anglo-Américaines." *H&M*, No. 107 (1955), pp. 450-452. [Review of Number 147. Interesting discussion of French critics' assessment of ED.]

626. Laverty, Carroll D. "Structural Patterns in Emily Dickinson's Poetry." *ESQ*, No. 44 (1966), 12-17. [ED's poems appear in at least eight basic structural patterns: (1) statement followed by an example or explanation, (2) parallelism, (3) analogy, (4) logical argument, (5) definition, (6) dramatic structure, (7) single statement, (8) combination of two or more of the above.]

627. Lavin, J. A. "Emily Dickinson and Brazil." *NEQ*, CCV (1960), 270-271. [Takes issue with Monteiro's definition of "Brazil" (Numbers 692, 693) in ED's "I asked no other thing" (J.621).]

628. Leary, Lewis. "The Poems of Emily Dickinson." *Thought* XXXI (1956), 282-286. [Generally favorable review of Number 47. Discusses previous editions, problems of editing, ED's punctuation.]

629. Lee, Anna Phillips. "Emily Dickinson and Her Family Tree." *DARM*, LXV (1931), 471-477.

630. Leyda, Jay. "Late Thaw of a Frozen Image." *NR*, CXXXII (21 Feb. 1955), 22-24. [Laments biographical errors that have become dogma and obscured true life.]

631. ———. *NEQ*, XXIX (1956), 239-245. [Reviews Number 47, applauding Johnson's editing generally but making several important objections and corrections.]

632. Lind, Sidney E. "Emily Dickinson's 'Further in Summer Than the Birds' and Nathaniel Hawthorne's 'Old Manse'." *AL*, XXXIX (1967), 163-169. [ED's poem (J.1068) may have been inspired by Hawthorne's essay.]

633. Lindberg, Brita. "Emily Dickinson's Punctuation." *SN*, XXXVII (1965), 327-359. [A thorough review of critics and editors' views on ED's punctuation, together with those of the poet herself. She used punctuation as an aspect of style.]

634. ———. "The Theme of Death in Emily Dickinson's Poetry." *SN*, XXXIV (1962), 269-281. [Lists general characteristics of ED's treatment of death. Death linked to religious considerations.]

635. ———. *SN*, XXXV (1963), 170-172. [Favorable review of Number 170.]

636. Lindquist, Ebba. "Emily Dickinson Efter Många År." *Oob*, LV (1946), 581-585.

637. Link, Franz H. "Vier Gedichte Emily Dickinson." *NS*, No. 9 (1954), pp. 406-413. [In German.]
638. Lubbock, Percy. "Determined Little Anchoress." *N&A*, XXXVI (1924), 114. [Review of Number 35. Finding ED personally vain, notes that this tendency led her to ignore poetic rules and flaw a large portion of her poetry. Lubbock, however, regards much of her work as brilliant. Reprinted in Number 174, pp. 118-120.]
639. Lynen, John F. "Three Uses of the Present: The Historian's, the Critic's, and Emily Dickinson's." *CE*, XXVIII (1966), 126-136. [The historical and critical approaches to literature can be reconciled by study of time as poetic method. Investigates ED's attitudes toward time, compares with those of Whitman.]
640. ———. *JEGP*, LXXII (1963), 421-426. [Review of Number 170.]
641. Mabbott, T. O. "'Boanerges' a Horse?" *AN&Q*, II (1963), 57. [A reply to Number 438 concerning J.585.]
642. McCarthy, Paul. "An Approach to Dickinson's Poetry." *ESQ*, No. 44 (1966), 22-31. [Pedagogical: explains how ED is taught to students at the Univ. of Alabama.]
643. McCausland, Elizabeth. "Emily Dickinson Born One Hundred Years Ago." *SpringR*, 4 May 1930. [An account of centennial celebration at Hampshire Bookshop. Reprinted in Number 10, pp. 29-36.]
644. McElderry, B. R., Jr. "Emily Dickinson: Viable Transcendentalist." *ESQ*, No. 44 (1966), 17-21. [ED is a Transcendentalist; her differences from Emerson are those of technique, not ideology.]
645. McKay, Margery. "'Amazing Sense': The Application of a New Method to the Poetry of Emily Dickinson." Swarthmore College [Honors Thesis], 1936. [Commended by Whicher (Number 211) and by Herbert E. Childs (Num-

ber 468). Sketches relationship between ED and Sir Thomas Browne. Vocabulary study.]

646. MacLean, Kenneth. "The Mail from *Tunis*." *UTQ*, xx (1950), 27-32. [Hypothesizes that ED identified herself with Cleopatra, and that the love story is implicit in the background of her poetry.]

647. McLean, Sydney R. "Emily Dickinson." *MHAQ*, xix (1936), 221-223. [Reviews Number 39.]

648. ———. "Emily Dickinson at Mount Holyoke." *NEQ*, vii (1934), 25-42. [Uses various school documents, letters, to reconstruct ED's contact with curriculum, politics, teachers, daily happenings. Emphasizes spiritual conflict.]

649. ———. *AL*, xvii (1946), 363-365. [Review of Numbers 51, 171. Plea for definitive text.]

650. McNally, James. "Perspectives in Movement: A Poem by Emily Dickinson." *CEA*, xxvi, No. 2 (1963), 9-10. [Explicates "I like to see it lap the miles" (J.585).]

651. McNaughton, Ruth Flanders. "Emily Dickinson on Death." *PrS*, xxiii (1949), 203-214. [Classifies and notes characteristics of death poems.]

652. Maguire, C. E. "Two Poets: Compared and Contrasted." *Thought*, viii (1933), 396-409. [ED and Katherine Tynan.]

653. Manierre, William R. "E. D.: Visions and Revisions." *TSLL*, v (1963), 5-16. [Compares original versions of "Because I could not stop for death" (J.712), "I heard a fly buzz when I died" (J.465), and "The soul selects her own society" (J.303) with edited versions to illustrate the value of Johnson's text (Number 47).]

654. Manley, Francis. "An Explication of Dickinson's 'After Great Pain'." *MLN*, lxxiii (1958), 260-264. [Irony is poem's aim and technique. Reprinted in Number 178, pp. 52-55.]

655. Marcellino, Ralph. "Cato and Emily Dickinson." *COut*, XXXV (1958), 55-56.

656. ———. "Dickinson's 'The Snow That Never Drifts'." *Expl*, XIII (1955), Item 36. [Reprinted in Number 314, p. 77.]

657. ———. "Emily Dickinson." *CE*, VII (1945), 102-103. [In "The only news I know" (J.827), "bulletins from Immortality" signifies news of death, not of God.]

658. ———. "Emily Dickinson." *NYHTB*, XII (3 May 1936), 22. [A note on the text of "Her grace is all she has" (J.810).]

659. ———. "Emily Dickinson's 'Ablative Estate'." *CJ*, LIII (1958), 231-232. [Explicates "That it will never come again" (J.1741).]

660. ———. "Horace and Emily Dickinson." *CJ*, L (1954), 126; LII (1957), 221-222.

661. ———. "Simonides and Emily Dickinson." *CJ*, XLII (1946), 140.

662. Marcus, Mordecai. "Dickinson's 'Not with a Club the Heart is Broken'." *Expl*, XX (1962), Item 54. [Reprinted in Number 314, pp. 73-74.]

663. ———. "Walt Whitman and Emily Dickinson." *Person*, XLIII (1962), 497-514. [Concentrates on similarities in views on function of poetry, on immortality, on man's purpose in life, on religion, and nature. Finds parallels in sense of personal frustration, adoption of masks, histories of publication and reception.]

664. Martz, Louis L. "Donne and the Meditative Tradition." *Thought*, XXXIV (1959), 269-278. [Brief mention.]

665. ———. *UTQ*, XXVI (1957), 556-565. [Review of Number 47. Partially reprinted in Number 277.]

666. Mary Humiliata, Sister. "Emily Dickinson—Mystic Poet?" *CE*, XII (1950), 144-149. [ED is found not to fall

within traditional definition of mysticism. Partially reprinted in Number 178, pp. 75-81.]

667. Matchett, William H. "Dickinson's Revision of 'Two Butterflies Went Out at Noon'." *PMLA*, LXX (1962), 436-441.

668. ———. "The 'Success' by Emily Dickinson." *BPLQ*, VIII (1956), 144-147. [Discusses editorial changes in "Success is counted sweetest" (J.67), as poem appeared in Number 67.]

669. ———. *MLQ*, XXII (1961), 91-94. [Review of Numbers 44, 170.]

670. Matthiessen, F. O. "The Problem of the Private Poet." *KR*, VII (1945), 584-597. [Reviews Numbers 51, 171. Of Number 171, regrets Bingham's determination to vindicate mother. Would prefer only details concerning publication. Commends chapter on Todd and Higginson's editing. Of Number 51, laments grouping is not chronological, but generally commends new edition. Related ED to Emerson, denies influence of metaphysical poets. Reprinted as "The Private Poet: Emily Dickinson," in *Responsibilities of the Critic: Essays and Reviews*, pp. 80-92. John Rackliffe, ed. New York: Oxford University Press, 1952; Number 174, pp. 224-235.]

671. Maurin, Mario. *NEQ*, XXXII (1959), 99-102. [Review of Number 46. Critical discussion of letters, general praise for editors.]

672. Maurois, André. "Emily Dickinson: Poétesse et Recluse." *RdP*, LX (1954), 1-13. [Primarily biographical, concentrating on ED's masters and her approach to death and immortality. Reprinted in Maurois' *Robert et Elizabeth Browning: Portraits suivis de Quelques Autres*, pp. 45-64. Paris: Bernard Gasset, 1955.]

673. Maynard, Theodore. "The Mystery of Emily Dickinson."

CathW, CXXXIV (1931), 70-81. [Reviews Numbers 36, 198. Speculates on identity of ED's "lover." Views poetry as naïve, quaint, limited in technical range.]

674. M. D. Z. [Zabel, Morton Dauwen]. "Christina Rossetti and Emily Dickinson." *Poetry*, XXXVII (1931), 213-216. [Sees similarity in that both went into seclusion as a result of religious experience, both turned to poetry. Does not, however, minimize differences.]

675. Merchant, Frank. "The Dickinson Mystery." *T&G*, I (Oct., 1930), 34-39. [Review of Numbers 198, 205.]

676. Meredith, William. *NEQ*, XXIX (1956), 252-254. [Generally favorable review of Number 40.]

677. Merideth, Robert. "Dickinson's 'I Had Not Minded Walls'." *Expl*, XXIII (1964), Item 25. [Discussed in Number 17.]

678. ———. "Emily Dickinson and the Acquisitive Society." *NEQ*, XXXVII (1964), 435-452. [Examines ED's social criticism of Age of Enterprise, focusing on diction of commerce, device of merchant, theme of loss and gain, minister as tradesman. Explications. Discussed in Number 18.]

679. Metzger, Charles R. "Emily Dickinson's Shy Bird." *ESQ*, No. 44 (1966), 21-22. [Explicates "A bird came down the walk" (J.328); the poem combines the accurate observations of a naturalist and the wit of the poet.]

680. Miles, Susan. "The Irregularities of Emily Dickinson." *LonMerc*, XIII (1925), 145-150, 157-158 [A wise and entertaining essay forming a reply to Number 690. Investigates relationship between ED's themes and kinds of rhyme employed. Concludes that ED used disjointed rhyme to reflect a disjointed universe. Hence, her bending of rhymes always had artistic purpose. Reprinted in Number 174, pp. 123-129.]

681. Miller, Betty. "Elizabeth and Emily Elizabeth." *TC*, CLIX

(1956), 574-583. [Review of Number 47, comparing ED with Elizabeth B. Browning regarding their seclusion, attachment to fathers, letter-writing, excessive fear for death of family or friends.]

682. Miller, F. DeWolfe. *NEQ*, XXXIV (1961), 114-116. [Review of Number 170.]

683. Miller, James E., Jr. "Emily Dickinson: The Thunder's Tongue." *MinnR*, II (1962), 289-304. [Definition of ED's aesthetics based on several poems. Examination of ED's revisions to determine artistic goals.]

684. ———. "Emily Dickinson's Bright Orthography." *HR*, XIV (1961), 301-306. [Review of Numbers 44, 170, 190.]

685. Miller, Perry. "Emily Dickinson: The Shunning of Joy." *Reporter*, XVIII (29 May 1958), 34-36. [Reviews Number 46, applauding Johnson, briefly discussing biographical implications of letters.]

686. ———. *NEQ*, XXIX (1956), 101-103. [Appreciative review of Number 188.]

687. Mills, Rosamund. "Emily Dickinson." *Interludes*, VII (1930-1931), 80-84.

688. Miner, Earl Roy. "Dickinson's 'A Clock Stopped—Not the Mantel's'." *Expl*, XIII (1954), Item 18. [Reprinted in Number 314, pp. 57-58.]

689. Moldenhauer, Joseph J. "Emily Dickinson's Ambiguity: Notes on Technique." *ESQ*, No. 44 (1966), 35-44. [Irony, paradox, and ambiguity are fundamental principles in ED's poetry.]

690. Monro, Harold. "Books of the Quarter." *Criterion*, III (1925), 322-324. [Review of Number 28. ED was ungrammatical, poorly educated, insensitive to language. Her few good poems were accidents. For a reply, see Number 680. Reprinted in Number 174, pp. 120-122.]

691. Montale, Eugenio. "Emily." *CdS*, IV (1957).

692. Monteiro, George. "Emily Dickinson and Brazil." *N&Q*, CCVII (1962), 312-313. [Takes issue with Number 627 concerning ED's use of "Brazil" in "I asked no other thing" (J.621).]

693. ———. "Emily Dickinson's Merchant God." *N&Q*, CCIV (1959), 455-456. [Explicates "I asked no other thing" (J.621). For a reply, see Number 627. Monteiro continues argument in Number 692.]

694. ———. "Traditional Ideas in Dickinson's 'I Felt a Funeral in My Brain!' " *MLN*, LXXV (1960), 656-663. [Relates poem philosophically to Emerson and Milton.]

695. Moore, Marianne. *Poetry*, LXI (1933), 219-226. [Complimentary review of Number 53. General assessment of ED.]

696. Moore, Virginia. "The Poetic Mind." *VQR*, XV (1939), 452-456. [Favorable review of Number 211.]

697. ———. "Women Poets." *Bookman*, LXXI (1930), 388-395. [Impressionistic assessment of ED's stature among women poets.]

698. Moran, Helen. " 'Queens, Now'." *LonMerc*, XXVI (1932), 138-146. [Review of Number 53. Impressionistic discussion of ED, Jane Austen, George Sand, E. B. Browning, Charlotte Brontë, Louisa Alcott.]

699. Moseley, Edwin. "The Gambit of Emily Dickinson." *UKCR*, XVI (1949), 11-19. [Finds source of ED's modernity in her mask of innocence, ironic distance. Examines this tone in her poetic treatment of nature, reason, God.]

700. Murciaux, Christian. "Emily Dickinson." *CS*, LI (1961), 276-289. [Primarily biographical, emphasizing ED's love for George Gould, Kate Anthon, Sue Dickinson. Critical comments on ED's use of Bible, relationship to mysticism, her poetic diction. In French.]

701. ———. "El Genio Puritano en el Siglo XIX: Ralph Waldo Emerson, Emily Dickinson, Walt Whitman." *Sur*, xx (Sept. and Oct., 1952), 84-108. [Considers impact of Civil War, religious heritage, use of Bible, mystical qualities. In Spanish.]

702. Nakao, Kiyoaki. "Emily Dickinson's 'Irreverence'." *ALR*, xix (1957), 5-8.

703. ———. "Studies in American Poetry: The Individuality of Emily Dickinson." *ScienR*, vi (1957), 1-12.

704. Newell, Kenneth B. "Dickinson's 'Aurora Is the Effort'." *Expl*, xx (1961), Item 5. [Reprinted in Number 314, pp. 56-57.]

705. ———. "Dickinson's 'We Should Not Mind So Small a Flower'." *Expl*, xix (1961), Item 65. [Reprinted in Number 314, p. 86.]

706. Nguyen-Khúc-Nha. "Emily Dickinson and the Renascence of Poetry in the United States." *CMR*, xiii (1964), 131-135, 294-306. [In Vietnamese.]

707. Niemeyer, Carl A. "The Gentleman with the Deep Voice." *UCR*, xlvii, iv (1958), 6-8. [Wadsworth.]

708. Niikura, Toshikazu. "Emily Dickinson's 'If You Were Coming in the Fall'." *MGR*, No. 73 (Nov., 1962), pp. 139-150.

709. ———. " 'Honest Doubt': Emily Dickinson's Religious Poetry." *MGR*, Nos. 64-65 (Oct., 1961), pp. 101-116.

710. ———. " 'Summer Poems' by Emily Dickinson." *ALR*, xxxiv (1961), 11-12.

711. Nist, John. "Dois Poetas Norte-Americanos e Uma Aranha." *Anhembi*, xxxv (1959), 480-484. [Comparison of Whitman and ED focusing on Dickinson's "A spider sewed at night" (J.1138) and Whitman's "A noiseless patient spider." In Portuguese. For a reprint in English see *WWBB*, iv (1961), 8-11.]

712. Noda, Hisashi. "Emily Dickinson's Poetry: An Essay on the Symbols of 'Death'." *KAL*, No. 6 (April, 1963), pp. 23-29. [In English.]

713. ———. "Notes on Emily Dickinson." *KAL*, No. 5 (April, 1962), pp. 63-70.

714. ———. "Notes on *This Was a Poet: A Critical Biography of Emily Dickinson* by G. F. Whicher (1938)." *KAL*, No. 9 (July, 1966). [Comment on Number 211. In English.]

715. Nogami, Akira. "E. Dickinson." *AmerB* (March, 1949).

716. North, Jessica Nelson. "Building a Legend." *Poetry*, XXXV (1929), 164-167. [Reviews Number 34 finding poems inferior to those of previous volumes. ED's prime fault is excessive economy.]

717. O'Brien, Anthony. "Emily Dickinson: The World, the Body, and the Reflective Life." *MCR*, No. 9 (1966), 69-80.

718. Ochshorn, Myron. "Dickinson's 'I Know Some Lonely Houses off the Road'." *Expl*, XI (1952), Item 12. [Reprinted in Number 314, pp. 66-67.]

719. ———. "In Search of Emily Dickinson." *NMQ*, XXIII (1953), 94-106. [Reviews Numbers 177, 195. Dismisses Patterson's biography (Number 195) as speculative. Accuses Chase (Number 177) of inept criticism and of a reworking of ideas by Whicher (Number 211) and Tate (Number 828). Maintains theme of suffering takes precedence over themes of death, immortality. Several explications.]

720. O'Connor, William Van. "The Responsibilities of Editors." *Poetry*, LXXIX (1952), 291-292. [Takes exception to Friar and Brinnin's explication (Number 243) of "Wonder is not precisely knowing" (J.1331).]

721. Omoto, Tsuyoshi. "Emily Dickinson's Poem 'No Rack Can Torture Me'." *HSELL*, IX, i-ii (June, 1963), 45-50.

722. Onís, Harriet de. "Emily Dickinson." *Asomante*, XII, ii (1956), 23-38. [Biography, history of publication, literary reputation, religion, views on death and immortality, impact of Civil War, technique. Several translations. In Spanish.]
723. Oppens, Kurt. "Emily Dickinson: Uberlieferung und Prophetie." *Merkur*, XIV (1960), 17-40. [Compares ED to Rilke.]
724. Pagnini, Marcello. "La Poesie di Emily Dickinson." *SA*, VIII (1962), 35-53.
725. Parker, Barbara N. "The Dickinson Portraits by Otis A. Bullard." *HLB*, VI (1952), 133-137. [Description and reproduction of paintings together with biographical sketch of their artist.]
726. Parks, Edd Winfield. "The Public and the Private Poet." *SAQ*, LVI (1957), 480-485. [Contrasts ED and Whitman's attitudes toward religion, function of poet, sex. Views Whitman as public, ED as private poet.]
727. Parsons, Thornton H. "The Indefatigable Casuist." *URev*, XXX (1963), 19-25. [Explicates poems illustrating various treatments of the theme of deprivation.]
728. Patee, Fred Lewis. "Gentian, Not Rose: The Real Emily Dickinson." *SR*, XLV (1937), 180-197. [Useful discussion of ED's literary reputation, focusing on various editions and their reception.]
729. Patterson, Rebecca. "Elizabeth Browning and Emily Dickinson." *EL*, XX (July, 1956), 21-48.
730. ———. "Emily Dickinson's Hummingbird." *EL*, XXII (1958), 12-19. [Explicates "A route of evanescence" (J.1463), focusing on literary allusion, imagery, symbolism, prosody. Reprinted in Number 178, pp. 140-148.]
731. ———. "Emily Dickinson's Palette." *MQ*, V (1964), 271-291; VI (1964), 97-117. [Part I is a thorough chron-

ological study of ED's developing use of color imagery in poetry and letters. Considers influence of Emerson and Elizabeth Browning. Part II is an analysis of use of green, blue, yellow, purple, red. ED's use of color imagery is emblematic of her emotional state. Both parts of the article are discussed in Number 17.]

732. Pearce, Roy Harvey. "On the Continuity of American Poetry." *HudR*, x (1957-58), 518-539. [Compares Emerson, Poe, Whitman, ED. All employ variations of the egocentric style, a self-sufficiency of thought and technique basic to American nineteenth-century verse. For book-length amplification, see Number 283.]

733. Perkinson, Grace E. "Emily Dickinson and Children." *HornBk*, XXXIII (Feb., 1957), 19-27. [Recommends ED as reading for children. Discusses ED's own childlike qualities and her friendships with children.]

734. Perrine, Laurence. "Dickinson's 'A Clock Stopped . . .'." *Expl*, XIV (1955), Item 4. [Reprinted in Number 314, p. 59.]

735. ———. "Dickinson's 'I Started Early Took My Dog'." *Expl*, x (1952), Item 28. [Reprinted in Numbers 178, pp. 88-89; 314, p. 69.]

736. ———. "Dickinson's 'My Life Had Stood a Loaded Gun'." *Expl*, XXI (1962), Item 21.

737. ———. "Dickinson's 'There's a Certain Slant of Light'." *Expl*, XI (1953), Item 50. [Reprinted in Numbers 178, pp. 34-35; 314, p. 80.]

738. ———. "Emily Dickinson's 'Presentiment' Again." *AN&Q*, III (1965), 119. [Takes exception with Number 572. Maintains that "Presentiment is that long shadow on the lawn" (J.764) is a definition poem attempting only to define term and not treat the subject of death. For a reply, see Number 574.]

739. ———. "Emily's Beloved Friend." *SWR*, XXXVII (1952), 81-83. [Reviews Number 195, finding credible the theory that Kate Scott Anthon was ED's love.]
740. ———. "The Importance of Tone in the Interpretation of Literature." *CE*, XXIV (1963), 389-395. [Explicates "Two butterflies went out at noon." (J.533).]
741. ———. "The Nature of Proof in the Interpretation of Poetry." *EJ*, LI (1962), 393-398. [Explicates "Where ships of purple gently toss" (J.265).]
742. Perry, Ernestine C. "Anecdotes of Noted Amherst Women Related." *SpringU*, 23 March 1929.
743. ———. "Mme. M. D. Bianchi Tells of a Vivid Emily Dickinson." *SpringU*, 24 Oct. 1930, p. 10.
744. Pineda, Rafael. "Emily Dickinson." *RNC*, Nos. 156-157 (Jan.-April, 1963), pp. 132-145.
745. Poetry Workshop, Columbus, Ga. "Dickinson's 'My Life Had Stood—A Loaded Gun'." *Expl*, XV (1957), Item 51. [Reprinted in Number 314, pp. 71-72.]
746. Pohl, Frederick J. "Dickinsoniana." *SatR*, VII (10 Jan., 1931), 522. [Corrects some factual errors in Number 205.]
747. ———. "The Emily Dickinson Controversy." *SR*, XLI (1933), 467-482. [Reviews theories concerning identity of ED's lover, finally favoring Major Hunt.]
748. ———. "The Poetry of Emily Dickinson." *AmhMo*, XXV (1910), 47-50.
749. Pollitt, Josephine. "Emily and Major Hunt." *SatR*, VI (5 July 1930), 1180. [Attempts to defend her position (Number 198) that Major Hunt was ED's love.]
750. Pommer, Henry F. "Dickinson's 'The Soul Selects Her Own Society'." *Expl*, III (1945), Item 32. [Reprinted in Number 314, p. 78.]
751. Porter, David T. "Emily Dickinson: The Formative

Years." *MR*, VI (1965), 559-569. [ED was already confident poet by the time she sought Higginson's advice. Discussion of ED's aesthetic as it emerged in letters and poems sent to Higginson. Several explications. Revised reprint in Number 199. Discussed in Number 18.]

752. ———. *NEQ*, XXXVI (1963), 522-524. [Appreciative review of Number 203.]

753. Praz, Mario. "Emily Dickinson." *La Stampa*, 10 Aug. 1939. [Reprinted in *Cronache Letterarie Anglosassoni*, v. II, pp. 149-152. Rome: Edizioni di Storia e Letteratura, 1951. In Italian.]

754. ———. "Voci di Poesia Dall'est e Dall'ovest." *Tempo*, 9 Oct. 1949. [Reprinted in *Cronache Letterarie Anglosassoni*, v. II. Rome: Edizioni di Storia e Letteratura, 1951. In Italian.]

755. Price, Warwick James. "The Poetry of Emily Dickinson." *YLM*, LIX (1893), 25-27.

756. ———. "Three Forgotten Poetesses." *Forum*, XLVII (1912), 361-366. [Other poets are Amy Levy and Emma Lazarus.]

757. Rabe, Olive H. "Emily Dickinson as Mystic." *CQ*, XIV (1966), 280-288. [Symbols of illumination and marriage, as well as poems of despair, clarify ED's importance as mystical poet.]

758. Raine, Kathleen. "The Little Emily." *NS&N*, XLIII (1952), 470-472. [Review of Number 53, viewing ED as over-rated eccentric of limited poetic distinction.]

759. Ransom, John Crowe. "Emily Dickinson: A Poet Restored." *PUSA*, No. 15 (1956), pp. 5-20. [Reviews Number 47, reproducing with commentary ten poems. Biographical detail. Reprinted in Number 203, pp. 88-100.]

760. Rapin, René. "Dickinson's 'Farther in Summer Than the Birds'." *Expl*, XII (1954), Item 24. [Reprinted in Numbers 178, pp. 127-129; 314, pp. 61-62.]

761. Read, Sir Herbert. "The Range of Emily Dickinson." *Spec*, CLI (1933), 971. [Review of Number 36. Falsely considers the collection complete and well-edited. Finds the poems dull, trite, repetitive. Reprinted in Number 174, pp. 173-175.]

762. Reid, Mary J. "Julia C. R. Dorr and Some of Her Poet Contemporaries." *MM*, III (1895), 499.

763. Riese, Teut Andreas. "Emily Dickinson und der Sprachgeist Amerikanischer Lyrik." *NS*, No. 3 (1963), pp. 145-159. [Discussed in Number 16.]

764. ———. "Das Gestaltungsprinzip der Konkretion in der Neueren Amerikanischen Lyrik." *JA*, No. 8 (1963), pp. 136-147. [The treatment of nature by ED, Thoreau, and Frost relative to each writer's use of the abstract and concrete. In German.]

765. Rizzardi, Alfredo. "Letteratura Anglo-Americana." *Conv*, N.S. XXXI (1963), 368-370. [In Italian.]

766. ———. "La Poesia di Melville." *SA*, I (1955). [Reprinted in *La Condizione Americana*. Bologna: Cappelli, 1960.]

767. Roach, H. "Emily Dickinson: A Heading." *ICUT*, XIII (1965), 185. [Pedagogical.]

768. Root, E. Merrill. "Clothes vs. Girl." *Measure*, No. 39 (1924), pp. 15-18. [Review of Number 35.]

769. ———. "Emily Dickinson: Symbol and Dynamo." *ChriCent*, L (1933), 784-786. [Like Poe, Thoreau, Whitman, Melville, ED was out of step with nineteenth century American society. Her response was the creation of a rich inner life.]

770. Rosenbaum, S. P. "Emily Dickinson and the Machine." *SB*, XVIII (1965), 207-227. [An account of Rosenbaum's use of the computer in preparing a concordance to ED (Number 202). Discussed in Number 17.]

771. Rosenberger, Coleman. "The Rediscovery of Emily Dickinson." *QQ*, LII (1945), 352-355. [Reviews Numbers 51, 171, recounting the history of the editing of ED MSS.]
772. Rossky, William. "Dickinson's 'A Clock Stopped . . .'." *Expl*, XXII (1963), Item 3. [Discussed in Number 16.]
773. Russell, Robert W. "Dickinson's 'At Half Past Three a Single Bird'." *Expl*, XVI (1957), Item 3. [Reprinted in Number 314, pp. 55-56.]
774. Sapir, Edward. "Emily Dickinson: A Primitive." *Poetry*, XXVI (1925), 97-105. [Review of Numbers 32, 35.]
775. Satterwhite, Joseph N. "Robert Penn Warren and Emily Dickinson." *MLN*, LXXI (1956), 347-349. [Compares Warren's explication (Number 228) of "After great pain a formal feeling comes" (J.341) with a parallel scene in Warren's novel, *All the King's Men.*]
776. Schappes, Morris U. "Book Reviews." *Sym*, I (1930), 545-550. [Generally favorable review of Number 205.]
777. ———. "Emily Dickinson." *SatR*, VIII (25 July 1931), 10. [Corrects factual errors in Number 282.]
778. ———. "Errors in Mrs. Bianchi's Edition of Emily Dickinson's *Letters*." *AL*, IV (1933), 369-384. [Bianchi's *Life and Letters* (Number 35) uses Mrs. Todd's 1894 edition as source, although most MSS were available. Schappes lists 68 mistakes in copying.]
779. ———. "Notes on the Concrete as Method in Criticism." *Sym*, II (1931), 318. [Explicates "Love is anterior to life" (J.917).]
780. ———. "An Obvious Error." *SatR*, VII (18 Oct. 1930), 256. [Corrects an error in Number 198 regarding the editing of a letter to Helen Hunt Jackson.]
781. ———. *Sym*, III (1932), 260-269. [Thorough review of Number 53. Brief but interesting comment on ED's stylistic development. Textual corrections.]

782. ———. *AL*, v (1933), 82-85. [Reviews Number 33. Finds frequent errors in fact, judgment, taste. New letters of little interest compared to rest of work.]

783. Schauffler, Henry Park. "The Second Edition of Emily Dickinson's Poems." *ALM*, vi (1891), 175-182. [Review of Number 55.]

784. ———. "Suggestions from the Poems of Emily Dickinson." *ALM*, vi (1891), 87-90.

785. Schlauch, Margaret. "Linguistic Aspects of Emily Dickinson's Style." *PF*, xviii (1963), 201-215.

786. Schreiber, Flora Rheta. "Emily Is in the House: Emily Dickinson as Revealed through Her Imagery." *PL*, XLVI (1940), 76-82. [Study of household imagery.]

787. Scott, Aurelia G. "Emily Dickinson's 'Three Gems'." *NEQ*, xvi (1943), 627-628. [Speculates that ED in a letter to Emmons, by listing pearl, onyx, and emerald stones, was thanking him for a volume of Poe.]

788. Scott, Wilbur. "Dickinson's 'I'll Tell You How the Sun Rose'." *Expl*, vii (1948), Item 14. [Reprinted in Number 314, pp. 67-68.]

789. Scott, Winfield Townley. "Emily Dickinson and Samuel Bowles." *Fresco*, x, No. 1 (1959), 7-17. [Assembles evidence to affirm the possibility that Bowles was ED's love. Admittedly speculative. Reprinted in *Fresco*, x, No. 3 (1960), 3-13; Scott's *Exiles and Fabrications*, pp. 40-49. Garden City, N. Y.: Doubleday and Company, Inc., 1961; "Errand from My Heart." *Horizon*, iii (1961), 100-105.]

790. Sedgwick, W. E. *NEQ*, ix (1936), 143-145. [Review of Number 39. Brief comparison of ED with Emerson and Melville.]

791. Sergeant, Elizabeth Shepley. "An Early Imagist." *NR*, iv (14 Aug. 1915), 52-54. [Review of Number 38, noting ED's relationship with the metaphysical poets, but deny-

ing direct influence. Finds source in Transcendentalism. Does not explore relationship with Imagists. Reprinted in Number 174, pp. 88-93.]

792. Sessions, Ruth Huntington. "Emily Dickinson Face to Face." *Nation*, CXXXVI (1933), 65-66. [Protests the search for ED's "lover."]

793. Sewall, Richard B. "Dickinson's 'To Undertake Is to Achieve'." *Expl*, VI (1948), Item 51. [Reprinted in Number 314, pp. 83-84.]

794. ———. "The Lyman Letters: New Light on Emily Dickinson and Her Family." *MR*, VI (1965), 693-780. [Adds to fund of biographical data. Contains description of ED and family written by Joseph B. Lyman (1829-1872), as well as nine quotations from letters ED wrote to him. Quotes excerpts from Lavinia and an entire letter from Austin. Sewall's editing is excellent, notes extensive. Reprinted as a monograph by University of Massachusetts, Amherst, 1965. Reviewed in Number 360. Discussed in Number 18.]

795. ———. "On Teaching Emily Dickinson." *ELeaf*, LXIII (1964), 3-14. [ED's reverence for the word, connotation, economy. Her mode is apprehension of truth through wit and metaphor. Explications.]

796. ———. *NEQ*, XVIII (1945), 409-411. [Review of Number 51. Commends editing, but finds poems of disappointing quality.]

797. Sexton, Carol. "The Relation of Emily Dickinson to God." *Aspects*, II, i (1965), 30-43. [Because human love relationships were denied her, ED took God as her lover.]

798. Shackford, Martha Hale. "The Poetry of Emily Dickinson." *Atlantic*, CXI (1913), 93-97. [Anticipates recent treatment of ED's intellect, humor, irony, imagery, use of paradox, and tragic qualities. Reprinted in Number 174,

pp. 79-88; Shackford's *Studies of Certain Nineteenth Century Poets*, pp. 75-82. Natick, Mass.: The Suburban Press, 1946.]

799. Sherrer, Grace B. "A Study of Unusual Verb Constructions in the Poems of Emily Dickinson." *AL*, vii (1935), 37-46. [Justifies ED's grammar. Deals with omission of auxiliaries, separation of subject and verb, subject-verb disagreements, etc. Irregular constructions are rare.]

800. ———. *AL*, xxiii (1951), 380-382. [Review of Number 59.]

801. ———. *AL*, xxiv (1952), 255-258. [Unfavorable review of Number 195.]

802. ———. *AL*, xxiv (1952), 407-410. [Reviews Number 177. Chapter on nature is prime accomplishment in book of consistently high quality.]

803. ———. *AL*, xxvii (1956), 598-600. [Favorable review of Number 40.]

804. Skeel, Esther Elizabeth. "Alumnae Conference Impressions." *MHAQ*, xiii (1930), 188-192.

805. Smidt, Aagot Karner. "Emily Dickinson." *Vinduet*, xv (1961), 220-223.

806. Smith, Grover. "Dickinson's 'A Route of Evanescence'." *Expl*, vii (1949), Item 54. [Reprinted in Numbers 178, pp. 138-139; 249.]

807. Smith, Russell St. Clair. "Dickinson's 'I Dreaded That First Robin So'." *Expl*, v (1947), Item 31. [Reprinted in Number 314, pp. 64-65.]

808. Spencer, Benjamin T. "Criticism: Centrifugal and Centripetal." *Criticism*, viii (1966), 141-142. [Explicates "I heard a fly buzz when I died" (J.465).]

809. Spencer, Theodore. *NEQ*, ii (1929), 498-501. [Review of Number 34, deploring editing. Discusses ED as metaphysical poet. Reprinted in Number 174, pp. 131-133.]

810. Spicer, John L ."The Poems of Emily Dickinson." *BPLQ*, VIII (1956), 135-143. [Favorable review of Number 47, giving some textual corrections.]

811. Spiller, Robert E. *MLN*, LXXIV (1959), 270-272. [Very favorable review of Number 46.]

812. Stamm, Edith Perry. "Emily Dickinson: Poetry and Punctuation." *SatR*, XLVI (30 March 1963), 23. [ED's seemingly unorthodox punctuation is part of standard elocutionary symbol system used in nineteenth century as guides to oral reading. For a reply, see Number 869. Partially reprinted in Number 178, pp. 59-64. Discussed in Number 16.]

813. Starke, Aubrey H. "Emily Dickinson as a Great Unknown." *ABC*, V (1934), 245-250. [Recounts history of Thomas Niles' publication of "Success Is Counted Sweetest" (J.67) in Number 67. See also Starke's Number 814.]

814. ———. "An Omnibus of Poets." *Colop* (1934), Pt. 16. [Gives history of *A Masque of Poets* (Number 67). Identifies other contributors, discusses critical reception.]

815. Stephenson, William E. "Emily Dickinson and Watt's Songs for Children." *ELN*, III (1966), 278-281. [ED's poetry owes a debt to Isaac Watt's *Divine Songs Attempted in Easy Language for . . . Children.*]

816. Stern, Milton R. "Poems for Teaching." *ClH*, XXXII (1958), 314-315. [Discusses imagery in "There's a certain slant of light" (J.258).]

817. Stevens, Harriet S. "Emily Dickinson y Juan Ramón Jiménez." *CHA*, LVI (1963), 29-49. [Discusses Juan Ramón's views of ED and his debt to her. Notes similarities in theme, imagery, form, language. Incidental comparisons with Béquer and Antonio Machado. Several explications. In Spanish.]

818. Stoddard, Francis H. "Technique in Emily Dickinson's

Poems." *The Critic*, xx (9 Jan. 1892), 24-25. [A reply to Number 388. Explicates "I died for beauty, but was scarce" (J.449) to illustrate ED's form is subtle but certainly present. Reprinted in Number 174, pp. 51-53.]

819. Stone, Edward. "Emily Dickinson's Collar." *Exercise Exchange*, XII (Nov. 1964), 3-4. [While not arguing for direct influence, notes similarities between Herbert's "The Collar" and ED's "I never lost as much but twice" (J.49).]

820. Sugden, Emily R. "Emily Dickinson." *SatR*, VII (13 Sept. 1930), 128. [Brief note expressing pleasure and interest in Amherst gossip regarding ED's lover.]

821. Swallow, Alan. *NMQ*, xv (1945), 222-224. [Appreciative review of Numbers 51, 171. ED as disciple of Emerson.]

822. Taggard, Genevieve. "Emily Dickinson." *Nation*, CXIX (1924), 376-378. [Unfavorable review of Numbers 32, 35.]

823. ———. "Emily Dickinson and Her Editor." *QRL*, II (1945), 350-353. [Reviews Numbers 51, 171. Finds quality of poems unequal to previous volumes. Discusses problems of editing.]

824. ———. "The Little 'Scholar' of 1848." *JAE*, II (1930), 75-76. [An account of Founders' Day celebration at Mount Holyoke.]

825. ———. "Notes on Emily Dickinson and Emerson." *SCM*, II (Nov. 1941), 3-6. [ED and Emerson as lyricists. While ED succeeds, Emerson fails because as an artist he is hampered by eighteenth-century form and as a man by lack of passion.]

826. Takaku, Shinichi. "Paradoxical Quality in Emily Dickinson's Poems." *JHGWJC*, No. 4 (1958), pp. 1-20.

827. Tate, Allen. "Emily Dickinson." *Outl*, CXLIX (1928), 621-623. [Important essay. Maintains that criticism failed

to realize that the source of ED's genius rests in her unconsciously Puritan world-view. Explores ED's tragic sense, relationship to Emerson, Hawthorne, James, Shakespeare, her technique, her emphasis on feeling as opposed to thought, her impact on American literature.]

828. ———. "New England Culture and Emily Dickinson." *Sym*, III (1932), 206-226. [Important essay viewing ED in her social and intellectual context. Puritanism gave her a fixed point of reference, while its disintegration impelled her toward egocentricity and poetry. Comparisons with Donne, Shakespeare, Hawthorne, Emerson, James. Reprinted as "Emily Dickinson" in Tate's *Reactionary Essays on Poetry and Ideas*, pp. 3-25. New York: Charles Scribner's Sons, 1936; Tate's *On the Limits of Poetry*, pp. 197-213. New York: Swallow Press and William Morrow and Company, 1948; *America through the Essay*, pp. 312-327. A. Theodore Johnson and Allen Tate, eds. New York: Oxford University Press, 1938; *Readings from the Americas*, pp. 232-246. Guy A. Cardwell, ed. New York: Ronald Press Company, 1947; Tate's *The Man of Letters in the Modern World: Selected Essays: 1928-1955*, pp. 211-226. New York: Meridian Books, 1955; *Allen Tate: Collected Essays*, pp. 197-213. Denver: Alan Swallow, Publisher, 1959; Numbers 162, pp. 84-111 (In Japanese); 174, pp. 153-167; 203, pp. 16-27. Partially reprinted in *Readings for Liberal Education*, vol. II, pp. 165-166. Louis G. Locke, ed. New York: Rinehart and Company, 1953; *Interpretations of American Literature*, pp. 204-205. Charles Feidelson, Jr. and Paul Brodtkorb, Jr., eds. New York: Oxford University Press, 1959; Numbers 178; 249.]

829. ———. "The Poet and Her Biographer." *KR*, I (1939), 200-203. [Review of Number 211.]

830. Tedeschi, Giuseppe. "Emily Dickinson Tra Critica e Leggenda." *FLe*, XV (31 Jan. 1960), 4.

831. Thomas, Macklin. "Analysis of the Experience in Lyric Poetry." *CE*, IX (1948), 317-321. [Pedagogical approach to "Go not too near a house of rose" (J.1434).]

832. Thomas, Owen Paul, Jr. "Dickinson's 'So Glad We Are'." *Expl*, XVIII (1959), Item 10. [Reprinted in Number 314, pp. 77-78.]

833. ———. *NEQ*, XXXIV (1961), 106-108. [Review of Number 190.]

834. ———. *NEQ*, XXXV (1962), 413-415. [Review of Number 209.]

835. Thompson, David W. "Interpretive Reading as Symbolic Action." *QJS*, XLII (1956), 395-396. [Discusses ritual, role, and gesture in "Go not too near a house of rose" (J.1434).]

836. Thompson, Maurice. "Miss Dickinson's Poems." *America*, V (1891), 425. [Review of Number 54, finding ED's poems interesting but marred by technical flaws. Reprinted in Number 174, pp. 28-33.]

837. Todd, Mabel Loomis. "About Authors." *BookB*, IX (Feb. 1892), 7. [Letter from Todd to editor stating that no picture of ED exists more recent than that taken in childhood.]

838. ———. "Emily Dickinson's Letters." *BA*, I (1895), 39-66. [Remarks on ED's development of prose style, her reading, seclusion, relationship to nature.]

839. ———. "Emily Dickinson's Literary Début." *HM*, CLX (1930), 463-471. [A personal account of Todd's friendship with ED, the editing of the MSS, the critics' reception of first edition (Number 54).]

840. Tolles, Catherine. "The Fire and Dew of Emily Dickinson." *MHAQ*, XXXVII (1930), 209-222. [ED as metaphysical poet.]

841. Tredant, Paul. "Lettre d'Amerique." *NL*, MXLIII (28 Aug. 1943), 2.

842. Trueblood, Charles K. "Emily Dickinson." *Dial*, LXXX (1926), 301-311. [Review of Number 35. Biographical and critical commentary. Brief comparison with Housman. Reprinted in *American Criticism*, pp. 291-307. William A. Drake, ed. New York: Harcourt, Brace and Company, 1926; *Literary Opinion in America*, pp. 251-262. Morton D. Zabel, ed. New York: Harper and Brothers, 1937. Not reprinted in Zabel's 2nd or 3rd eds.]

843. Tugwell, Simon. "Dickinson's 'The Crickets Sang'." *Expl*, XXIII (1965), Item 46.

844. ———"Notes on Two Poems by Emily Dickinson." *N&Q*, N.S. XIII (Sept., 1966), 342-343. [Explicates "Portraits are to daily faces" (J.170) and "Superfluous were the sun" (J.999).]

845. Turner, Arlin. "Emily Dickinson Complete." *SAQ*, LV (1956), 501-504. [Appreciative review of Number 47. Brief discussion of previous editions.]

846. ———. *SAQ*, LVIII (1959), 132-134. [Review of Number 46. New chronological grouping permits study of intellectual development. Uses changing attitudes toward church attendance and death as examples. Briefly discusses relationship between letters and verse.]

847. Tusiani, Giuseppe. "L'Italia nella Poesia di E. Dickinson." *PP*, No. 26 (Jan.-Feb., 1957).

848. Untermeyer, Louis. "Colossal Substance." *SatR*, V (16 March 1929), 769-771. [Comparison of ED and Christina Rossetti. Discussion of love theory. Review of Number 34.]

849. ———. "The Compleat Spinster Poet." *SatR*, XXXVIII (10 Sept. 1955), 37-39. [Appreciative review of Number 47. History of previous editions.]

850. ———. "Daughters of Niobe." *ASpec*, I (Nov., 1932), 4. [Observes tone of self-pity in ED's work and in that of other women poets.]

851. ———. "Emily Dickinson." *SatR*, VI (5 July 1930), 1169-1171. [Review of Numbers 187, 198, 205. Some praise for Taggard, none for Pollitt. Pleads for reliable text to form basis for definitive biography. Discusses various candidates for ED's lover, concluding that his identity is insignificant.]

852. ———. "Thoughts after a Centenary." *SatR*, VII (20 June 1931), 905-906. [A protest against the proliferation of love theories, lack of biographical data, unreliability of texts, the strange circumstances surrounding the ED portraits.]

853. Vacura, Zdenek. "The Discovery of Emily Dickinson's Poems." *Slovesná Veda*, I (1947), 31.

854. Van Der Vat, D. G. "Emily Dickinson (1830-1886)." *ES*, XXI (1939), 241-260. [Interesting treatment of ED's relationship to Puritanism, mysticism, and the metaphysical poets. Deals with nature poetry, death poetry, love poetry, and poetry which explores the mind. Comparison with Rilke, T. S. Eliot.]

855. Van Deusen, Marshall. "Dickinson's 'Farther in Summer Than the Birds'." *Expl*, XIII (1955), Item 33. [Reprinted in Numbers 178, pp. 129-131; 314, pp. 63-64.]

856. ———. "Dickinson's 'These Are the Days When Birds Come Back'." *Expl*, XII (1954), Item 40. [Reprinted in Numbers 178, pp. 3-4; 314, pp. 81-82.]

857. Van Doorn, Willem. "How It Strikes a Contemporary: Emily Dickinson." *ES*, VIII (1926), 132-135. [ED's poetry lacks technique.]

858. Van Doren, Mark. "The Mystery of Emily Dickinson." *TGM*, VII (Aug., 1930), 40-41.

859. ———. "Nerves Like Tombs." *Nation*, CXXVIII (20 March 1929), 348-349. [Reviews Number 34. Sees wit as the prime quality in ED's work. For an expanded version, see Number 309.]

860. Van Wyck, William. "Emily Dickinson's Songs out of Sorrow." *Person*, XVIII (1937), 183-189. [Appreciative, impressionistic.]

861. Vestdijk, Simon. "De Vlinder in de Kerk." *CrB* (July-Aug., 1939), pp. 214-216. [Reviews Number 211.]

862. Vickery, Gertrude. "Emily Dickinson: Famous Poetess." *AmhR*, 27 Nov., 1935, p. 2.

863. Vicuna, Magdalena. "Emily Dickinson." *AndQ* (Spring, 1946), pp. 16-20.

864. Voigt, Gilbert P. "The Inner Life of Emily Dickinson." *CE*, III (1941), 192-196. [Unscholarly treatment of ED as mystic. Comparison with St. Teresa.]

865. Waggoner, Hyatt H. "Emily Dickinson: The Transcendent Self." *Criticism*, VII (1965), 297-334. [Emerson's influence on ED's mind and art. Discussed in Number 18.]

866. Ward, Theodora. "Emily Dickinson and T. W. Higginson." *BPLQ*, V (1953), 3-18. [A thorough and reliable account. Reprinted in Number 209, pp. 178-196.]

867. ———. "The Finest Secret: Emotional Currents in the Life of Emily Dickinson after 1865." *HLB*, XIV (1960), 82-106. [Examines the quality and quantity of ED's letters, together with some poems, to discover the development of ED's mind during the years following her most productive period. Describes the effect of certain events, e.g., her father's death, on her art and philosophy. Reprinted in Number 209, pp. 78-112.]

868. ———. "Ourself Behind Ourself: An Interpretation of the Crisis in the Life of Emily Dickinson." *HLB*, X (1956), 5-39. [Examines representative poems year by year

through the highly creative period, 1858-1865. Declines to identify man who provoked the crisis. Personal conflict helped ED to regard poetry as art rather than therapy. Reprinted in Number 209, pp. 40-77.]

869. ———. "Poetry and Punctuation." *SatR*, XLVI (27 April 1963), 25. [Refutes Stamm (Number 812), pointing out ED used dashes in letters, where guides to oral reading were unnecessary. Also, frequency of dashes increases in period of emotional distress.]

870. Warren, Austin. "Emily Dickinson." *SR*, LXV (1957), 565-586. [Reviews Number 47, discussing previous editions and commending Johnson's text. Treats ED's punctuation, poetic development, relationship to Emerson, Isaac Watts, Sir Thomas Browne, her poetic vocabulary, use of Bible, her possible loves, her nature poetry, death poetry, and views on immortality. Reprinted in *American Critical Essays: Twentieth Century*, pp. 105-129. H. L. Beaver, ed. London: Oxford University Press, 1959; Numbers 174, pp. 268-286; 203, pp. 101-116.]

871. Waterman, Nixon. "Women Poets of America: Our 'Feminine Walt Whitman'." *BG*, 1 July 1924, p. 16.

872. Waugh, Dorothy. "Dickinson's 'Those Not Live Yet'." *Expl*, XV (1957), Item 22. [Reprinted in Number 314, pp. 82-83.]

873. ———. "Emily Dickinson: Horticulturalist." *Hort*, XXXII (1954), 367.

874. ———. "Emily Dickinson's Garden: Photos by Holbrook Clark." *PG*, IV, No. 1 (1953), 34-35, 68-70.

875. Wells, Anna Mary. "Further Poems of Emily Dickinson." *MHAQ*, XIII (1929), 78-81. [Reviews Number 34, finding poems of disappointing quality compared with those of previous editions.]

876. ———. "A Poet's Biography of a Poet." *MHAQ*, XIV (1930), 161-163. [Appreciative review of Number 205.]

877. ———. "Was Emily Dickinson Psychotic?" *AI*, XIX (1962), 309-321. [Hypothesizes that ED was psychotic in 1856-57 and never fully recovered.]

878. ———. *AL*, II (1931), 455-458. [Review of Numbers 10, 187, 198, 205. Dismisses Jenkins as anecdotal and unscholarly. Deals primarily with the biographies, condemning them for excessive conjecture but praising them in other respects. Regrets Hampson bibliography is incomplete.]

879. Wells, Carolyn. "Lavinia Dickinson." *Colop* (Sept., 1930), pt. 3. [Personal reminiscence of an interview with ED's sister.)

880. Wells, Henry W. *AL*, XXVIII (1956), 93-95. [Reviews Number 188, praising Johnson's judgment, organization, treatment of nature, analysis of rhythms, while mildly condemning his failure to study poetic development, provide psychological analysis, literary criticism.]

881. West, H. F. "Samuel F. Dickinson." *DAM*, XXVII (Feb., 1935).

882. West, Ray B., Jr. "Emily Dickinson's Forest." *RMR*, V (1941), 1-3. [A note on ED's use of insects.]

883. Wheatcroft, John. "Emily Dickinson's Poetry and Jonathan Edwards on the Will." *BuR*, X (1961), 102-127. [Edwards' Protestantism influenced ED's poetry in matter of theme, imagery, diction. Emphasizes Edwards' Lockean concept of will and necessity. Explores relationship between will and the creative process in selected ED poems.]

884. ———. "Emily Dickinson's White Robes." *Criticism*, V (1963), 135-147. [Investigates ED's use of white robes as metaphor in love poetry and death poetry. Examples and explications. Discussed in Number 16.]

885. Whicher, George F. "A Chronological Grouping of Some of Emily Dickinson's Poems." *Colop* (1934), Pt. 16. [An early attempt at dating, now superseded by Number 47.]

886. ———. "The Deliverance of Emily Dickinson, One of America's Greatest Poets." *NYHTB*, 13 Aug. 1950, Pt. 2, pp. 2, 12. [ED MSS given to Harvard; Thomas H. Johnson named editor.]

887. ———. "Emily Dickinson." *Cweal*, XXIX (1939), 297. [Defends his biography (Number 211) against brief review by Sister Rose Marie in *Cweal*, XXIX (1938), 106.]

888. ———. "Emily Dickinson: Centennial Afterthoughts." *AGQ*, XX (Feb., 1931), 94-99. [Reprinted in *In Other Words: Amherst in Prose and Verse*, pp. 123-128. Horace W. Hewlett, ed. Amherst, Mass.: Amherst College Press, 1964. General introd. to ED; sees her, in contrast to Whitman, as one who reflects the tragic aspects of her age.]

889. ———. "Emily Dickinson's Earliest Friend." *AL*, VI (1934), 3-17, 192-193. [Benjamin Franklin Newton, not Leonard Humphrey, is the "friend who taught me Immortality." Postscript answers Number 419, absolving Mrs. Todd of blame for ignoring Newton in the 1931 edition of Number 53. Some data on Mrs. Newton. Reprinted as Whicher's *Emily Dickinson's Earliest Friend.* Durham, N. C.: Duke University Press, 1934.]

890. ———. "Emily's Suitors." *Forum*, CVI (1946), 162-166. [Discussion of how biographical error is created through faulty reminiscence.]

891. ———. "In Emily Dickinson's Garden." *Atlantic*, CLXXVII (Feb., 1946), 64-70. [Attacks De Voto's Freudian analysis of ED (Number 503), maintaining ED is not poet of hatred. De Voto was misled by Number 171.]

892. ———. "Pursuit of the Overtakeless." *Nation*, CLXIX (2 July 1949), 14-15. [Interesting account of Whicher's interview with Wadsworth's son. Concludes ED's love for Wadsworth was unreciprocated. Reprinted in *Poetry and*

Civilization, pp. 63-69. Harriet Fox Whicher, ed. Ithaca, N. Y.: Cornell University Press, 1955; *In Other Words: Amherst in Prose and Verse*, pp. 141-144. Horace W. Hewlett, ed. Amherst, Mass.: Amherst College Press, 1964.]

893. ———. "Uriel in Amherst." *AGQ*, xxiii (1934), 281-292. [ED may have attended Emerson's Amherst lectures in 1855 and 1857, may even have met him at the Austin Dickinson home.]

894. ———. *AL*, iv (1932), 318-322. [Favorable review of Number 53, praising Mrs. Todd's faithful editing, corrections, addition of new letters, introduction, indexes. New edition sheds light on biographical problems, e.g., friendship with Wadsworth.]

895. ———. *AL*, xii (1940), 124-126. [Reviews Number 176, criticizing unreliable evaluations of previous scholarship, numerous factual errors, derivative treatment of Puritan background. Commends chapter on poetry itself.]

896. ———. *NEQ*, xvii (1944), 130-132. [Review of Number 201. Condemns book as propagandistic, filled with errors of fact and interpretation.]

897. ———. *NEQ*, xviii (1945), 261-264. [Review of Number 171. A humorous look at the Dickinson feud and Mrs. Todd's editing practices.]

898. Whicher, George M. "Emily Dickinson: A New England Mystic." *Land*, xiii (1931), 467-470. [Article is signed "George M. Whicher," but table of contents and index list "J. M. Whicher." Recounts known biographical detail with some inaccuracies.]

899. Whicher, Stephen. "Dickinson's 'Elysium Is As Far As To'." *Expl*, xix (1961), Item 45. [Reprinted in Number 314, p. 59.]

900. White, William. "Emily Dickinson." *TLS*, 2 March 1956, p. 133. [A letter praising Number 40.]

901. ———. "What Is a Collector's Item: Emily Dickinson, E. A. Robinson, D. H. Lawrence?" *ABC*, VI (1956), 6-8.

901a. ———. "Why Collect Ernest Hemingway—Or Anyone?" *PrS*, XL (1966), 232-246. [White collects ED books to facilitate his scholarly projects on the poet.]

902. Whiteside, Mary Brent. "Poe and Dickinson." *Person*, XV (1934), 315-326. [Comparison does not extend to technique. Finds similarities in emotional, self-revealing quality of poetry, in their themes, relations with society, egoism, worldview.]

903. W.I.F. "A Gifted Family." *Critic*, XXXII (1898), 359. [Personal reminiscence occasioned by death of Edward Dickinson, ED's nephew. Brief history of family.]

904. Wilder, Thornton. "Emily Dickinson." *Atlantic*, CXC (Nov., 1952), 43-48. [Interesting essay dealing with ED's coquettish, childish tone, finding its source in her strange relationship to her father. Maintains ED's best poetry transcends this tone or uses it masterfully. Commentary on ED's views of fame also noteworthy.]

905. Williams, Paul O. "Dickinson's 'One Day Is There of the Series'." *Expl*, XXIII (1964), Item 28. [For a conflicting interpretation, see Number 338. Discussed in Number 17.]

906. Williams, Stanley T. *MLN*, LXXII (1957), 64-66. [Favorable review of Number 188, briefly touching on ED's relations with friends and family.]

907. Willy, Margaret. "The Poetry of Emily Dickinson." *E&S*, X (1957), 91-104. [Compares ED with Emily Brontë. Finds many similarities, including their personalities, religious views, private lives, independence, and attitudes toward publication.]

908. Wilson, James Southall. "Emily Dickinson and Her Poems." *VQR*, XXXII (1956), 154-157. [Appreciative review of Numbers 40, 47, 188.]

909. ———. "Emily Dickinson and the 'Ghosts'." *VQR*, VI (1930), 624-630. [Review of Numbers 187, 205. Finds Taggard's biography slick but basically honest. Raises objections concerning style and structure. Praises Jenkins' work highly.]

910. ———. "Second Debut of Emily Dickinson." *VQR*, XXI (1945), 447-452. [Review of Numbers 51, 171. Appreciative of ED and Mrs. Bingham.]

911. Wilson, Suzanne M. "Emily Dickinson and Twentieth-Century Poetry of Sensibility." *AL*, XXXVI (1964), 349-358. [Notes similarity between ED's poetry and that of French Symbolists and Japanese haiku poets. Focuses on imagery and structure. Discussed in Number 17.]

912. ———. "Structural Patterns in the Poetry of Emily Dickinson." *AL*, XXXV (1963), 53-59. [Establishes ED as conscious artist by discovering a recurring structural plan: the three-part sermon. See Number 516 for criticism of this article. See also Number 16.]

913. Wingate, Charles E. L. "Boston Letter." *Critic*, XIX (1891), 141. [Brief comment regarding ED's relationship with T. W. Higginson.]

914. Winterich, John T. "Good Second-Hand Condition." *PW*, CXVIII (1930), 2311-2313. [Discusses "Success is counted sweetest" (J.67) as it appeared in *A Masque of Poets* (Number 130), gives biographical description of book, and mentions notations that T. W. Higginson made in his personal copy regarding textual changes.]

915. ———. "Two New Emily Dickinson Books." *PW*, CXLVII (1945), 1938-1942. [Generally favorable review of Numbers 51, 171. Briefly compares the Dickinsons with the Brontës.]

916. Wright, Nathalia. "Emily Dickinson's Boanerges and Thoreau's Atropos: Locomotives on the Same Line?"

MLN, LXXII (1957), 101-103. [Internal evidence of influence; external evidence lacking. Reprinted in Number 178, pp. 96-98.]

917. W. S. K. "A Fresh Reading of Emily Dickinson." *BET*, 11 July 1895, p. 5. [Appreciative comments.]

918. Yamamoto, Shuji. "Emily Dickinson and the Concept of Immortality." *KAL*, No. 4 (Sept. 1961), pp. 13-15. [In Japanese.]

919. ———. "Emily Dickinson: Person and Poetry." *KAL*, No. 3 (May, 1960), pp. 15-20.

920. Zolla, Elémire. "L'etica Puritana di Emily Dickinson." *SA*, VIII (1962), 54-70.

See also Numbers 22, 116.

VI. Doctoral Dissertations

921. Adams, Helen R. "The Prosody of Emily Dickinson." University of Pennsylvania, 1932.
922. Anselmo, Sister Peter Marie. "Renunciation in the Poems and Letters of Emily Dickinson." Notre Dame, 1965. [Considers ED's withdrawal from orthodox religion, marriage, fame, society. Studies impact on her work.]
923. Arp, Thomas Roscoe. "Dramatic Poses in the Poetry of Emily Dickinson." Stanford University, 1962. [Poems fail or succeed depending on ED's control over personae.]
924. Canan, Jessie E. "The Religion of Emily Dickinson." University of Pittsburgh, 1933.
925. Capps, Jack Lee. "Emily Dickinson's Reading, 1836-1886: A Study of the Sources of Her Poetry." University of Pennsylvania, 1963. [For a revised, published version, see Number 175. Discussed in Number 16.]
926. Copple, Lee B. "Three Related Themes of Hunger and Thirst, Homelessness, and Obscurity as Symbols of Privation, Renunciation, and Compensation in the Poems of Emily Dickinson." University of Michigan, 1954.
927. Di Salvo, Leta Perry. "The Arrested Syllable: A Study of the Death Poetry of Emily Dickinson." Univ. of Denver, 1965.
928. Ford, Thomas Wellborn. "The Theme of Death in the Poetry of Emily Dickinson." University of Texas, 1959. [Revised and published, see Number 181.]

928a. Frank, Bernhard. "The Wiles of Words: Ambiguity in Emily Dickinson's Poetry." Univ. of Pittsburgh, 1965. [ED produces ambiguity through a single word, through syntax, paradox, riddle, imagery, allusion.]

929. Franklin, Ralph William. "Editing Emily Dickinson." Northwestern University, 1965. [Covers 1886 to present. Careful checking of variorum edition (Number 47) reveals errors and omissions. Recommends revision.]

930. Gelpi, Albert Joseph. "The Business of Circumference: The Mind and Art of Emily Dickinson." Harvard University, 1962. [For a revised, published version, see Number 182.]

931. Granichstaedten-Czerva, Elisabeth. "Bildersprache bei Emily Dickinson." Vienna, 1940.

932. Gregor, Norman. "The Luxury of Doubt: A Study of the Relationship between Imagery and Theme in Emily Dickinson's Poetry." University of New Mexico, 1955. [ED is suspended between sterility and fulfillment; her poems develop a five-act drama of redemption, for which " 'Twas like a maelstrom with a notch" (J.414) is the model.]

933. Higgins, David James Monroe. "Portrait of Emily Dickinson: The Poet and Her Prose." Columbia University, 1961. [Biographical conclusions derived from study of letters. Partially reprinted in Number 203, pp. 162-177; *Twentieth Century Views*, pp. 162-177. N. Y.: Prentice-Hall, 1963. For a book-length, published version see Number 186.]

934. Jones, Rowena Revis. "Emily Dickinson's 'Flood Subject': Immortality." Northwestern University, 1960. [Views ED against Puritan background. Designates her as a poet of doubt.]

935. Keller, Karl. "The Metaphysical Strain in Nineteenth-Century American Poetry." University of Minnesota,

1964. [ED learned use of household imagery and juxtaposition of opposites from George Herbert.]

936. Kelly, Louise Kline. "A Concordance of Emily Dickinson's Poems." Pennsylvania State College, 1951. [Superseded by Number 202.]

936a. Kriesberg, Ruth Miller. "The Poetry of Emily Dickinson." New York University, 1965. [ED's style was formed as a consequence of Bowles' rejection of her as poet and person, and Higginson's advice that she remain unpublished.]

937. Lair, Robert Leland. "Emily Dickinson's Fracture of Grammar." Ohio State Univ., 1966.

938. Marcus, Mordecai. "Nature Symbolism in the Poetry of Emily Dickinson." University of Kansas, 1958.

939. Molson, Francis Joseph. "The 'Forms' of God: A Study of Emily Dickinson's Search for and Test of God." Notre Dame, 1965. [ED learned to substitute a powerful God for the elusive fatherly God.]

940. Porter, David Thomas. "The Art of Emily Dickinson's Early Poetry." University of Rochester, 1964. [Discussed in Number 17. For a revised and expanded version, see Number 199.]

941. Sherwood, William Robert. "Circumference and Circumstance: Stages in the Mind and Art of Emily Dickinson." Columbia University, 1964. [Studies influences and relationship between biography and poetic theme. Explicates numerous poems. Considers ED's use of solar and seasonal imagery.]

942. Thomas, Owen Paul, Jr. "The Very Press of Imagery: A Reading of Emily Dickinson." University of California at Los Angeles, 1959. [Traces artistic development through use of imagery.]

943. Todd, John Emerson. "Emily Dickinson's Use of the Per-

sona." University of Wisconsin, 1965. [Analyzes major personae: that of "little girl," the "lover-wife-queen," the dying or the dead, the inner self, and those resembling but distinct from ED herself. Discussed in Number 18.]

944. Wheatcroft, John Stewart. "Emily Dickinson and the Orthodox Tradition." Rutgers University, 1960. [See also Number 883.]

945. Wilson, Suzanne Marie. "Structure and Imagery Patterns in the Poetry of Emily Dickinson." University of Southern California, 1959. [See also Numbers 911 and 912.]

Index of Poetry Explications

Index of Authors